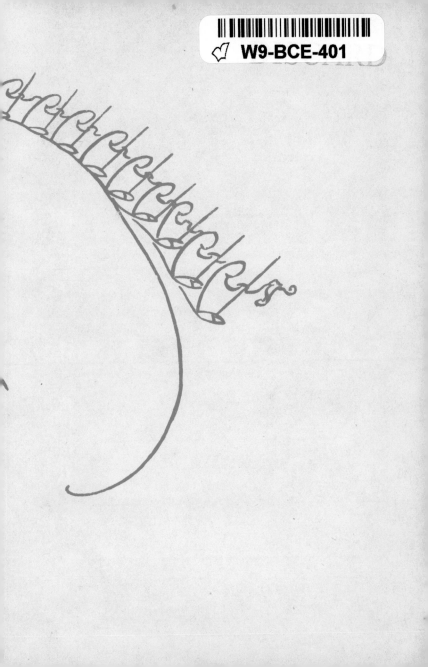

The Master Musicians

New Series Edited by Eric Blom

PALESTRINA

BACH ∽ Eva Mary and Sydney Grew
BEETHOVEN ∽ Marion M. Scott
BERLIOZ ∽ ∽ J. H. Elliot
BIZET ∽ ∽ Winton Dean
BRAHMS ∽ ∽ Peter Latham
CHOPIN ∽ ∽ Arthur Hedley
DEBUSSY ∽ Edward Lockspeiser
DVOŘÁK ∽ ∽ Alec Robertson
ELGAR ∽ ∽ W. H. Reed
FAURÉ ∽ Norman Suckling
GLUCK ∽ ∽ Alfred Einstein
HANDEL ∽ Percy M. Young
HAYDN ∽ Rosemary Hughes
LISZT ∽ ∽ Humphrey Searle
MENDELSSOHN John F. Waterhouse
MOZART ∽ ∽ Eric Blom
MUSSORGSKY ∽ M. D. Calvocoressi
PURCELL ∽ J. A. Westrup
RAVEL ∽ ∽ Norman Demuth
SCHUBERT ∽ Arthur Hutchings
SCHUMANN ∽ Joan Chissell
TCHAIKOVSKY ∽ Edwin Evans
VERDI ∽ ∽ Dyneley Hussey
WAGNER ∽ Robert L. Jacobs
WEBER ∽ William Saunders

Giovanj prenaloysio

The Master Musicians

PALESTRINA

by

HENRY COATES

Illustrated

London   J. M. Dent and Sons Ltd

J. M. DENT & SONS LTD.
Aldine House · Bedford St. · London

Made in Great Britain
by
The Temple Press · Letchworth · Herts.
First published 1938
Reprinted 1948

W 5/6 m

PREFACE

FOR the biographical portion of this book I have relied principally upon the works of Mgr. Casimiri (Director of Music at the Lateran basilica) and Signor Cametti (Musical Director of San Luigi dei Francesi in Rome), whose researches during the last twenty-five years have disclosed new and interesting facts concerning the composer.

It has not been possible, within the limits of this volume, to present anything like an exhaustive account of the vast mass of Palestrina's creative work, but I have attempted a general survey, with some description of works which seem most typical and outstanding examples of his musical style.

I have to thank those who assisted me in the preparation of this book: the Rev. G. H. Bishop, for kind help in various ways; Messrs J. & W. Chester Ltd. and Messrs. B. Feldman & Co. (representing the Breitkopf & Härtel edition), who were good enough to put scores at my disposal and to allow me to quote therefrom; and the Italian State Tourist Department, to whom I am indebted for some of the illustrations.

H. C.

LONDON,
February 1938.

CONTENTS

ILLUSTRATIONS

CHAPTER I

To a considerable part of the music-loving public Palestrina's name probably counts for little or nothing more than that of a medieval church composer who wrote a great quantity of music possessing mainly a religious and historical interest.

To say that his was one of the three or four greatest musical minds the world has ever known, and that his art has exercised a most profound influence upon the majority of the great composers who have followed him, might seem an exaggeration, were it not for the fact that the latter themselves, however diverse their musical creeds, have all acclaimed him as their equal, have even venerated him as master and teacher. He is above all a musician for the musicians: for them he is the master-craftsman in the art of working in sound.

Wagner and Brahms, Gluck and Mozart, Schumann and Liszt (who in his last years aspired to be known as 'the modern Palestrina'), Mendelssohn, Beethoven and even Debussy (in some of whose work the sixteenth-century influence is unmistakable)—these and many other composers of lesser rank have all testified to the spell which the old master's work cast over them. Wagner, who speaks for all in proclaiming the 'sublimity, richness and indescribable depth of expression' in Palestrina's music, probably learnt as much from the latter as he did from Liszt. If we look closely at the construction of such a work as the *Missa Aeterna Christi munera*, with its system of representative themes, passing from one movement to another, and remember that it was while at Dresden Wagner first became acquainted with this and many another Palestrinian masterpiece, making an intensive study of them all, we must come to the conclusion that the leading-motive system may well have been suggested to him by the musical style of the older master. It is, at any rate, a remarkable coincidence that Wagner's new ideas took shape just after the Dresden period.

Other instances of the influence Palestrina has exerted over creative musicians might be quoted. According to one of his biographers, Beethoven, while engaged on the composition of his own Mass, momentarily laid the work aside and began a study of Palestrina's masses, not, of course, to derive any actual ideas therefrom, but to steep himself in their spiritual, remote, impersonal atmosphere. Then we may recall Mendelssohn's description of the Holy Week music in Rome, where he speaks of the deep impression made on him by the *Improperia* and the *Lamentations*, 'the beautiful commencement of which,' he says, 'sounds as if it came direct from heaven.'

And there is the picture which Léon Vallas has drawn for us in his biography of Debussy of that composer leaving the church of Saint-Gervais in Paris after listening to some Palestrina: 'With a light in his eyes I have never seen before he came over to me exclaiming: "*That* is music." ' He goes on to tell us how Debussy's enthusiasm also took the form of playing the masses and motets as pianoforte duets with Paul Dukas.

Such illustrations could be multiplied: even Bach paid his tribute to the old Roman master, his homage taking the rather curious form of adding instrumental accompaniments [1] to the 'Kyrie' and 'Gloria' of the six-part Mass *Sine nomine* and performing them frequently in this form at St Thomas's in Leipzig.

[1] According to Félix Raugel.

The very inaccessibility of Palestrina's music has fostered the view suggested at the beginning of this chapter and prevented anything like a popular appreciation of his work, such as that of Bach or Beethoven enjoys. The average music-lover has but a very limited opportunity of hearing anything by Palestrina: his name occurs but seldom in concert programmes, and he alone of the great composers has escaped the sinister attentions of the arranger. The worst fate that has happened to him in this connection (a mild one compared to that of others) is the adaptation of some of the motets, and movements from the masses, to English words of an utterly unsuitable character, often diametrically opposed to the meaning of the original Latin.

The fullest acquaintance with Palestrina's music can only be made in the place and at the time for which it was intended —the liturgical services of the Roman Catholic church; and only under these conditions will it be fully understood, for it is art designed with a sole purpose, as part of the corporate worship of that church. Palestrina is indeed unique, in one sense, as a composer, for his is not the case of a genius deciding to devote himself to composing religious music, but rather of one whose art had its origin and inspiration in the church of which he was such a devoted son, and to which he gave a liturgical treasure such as no other musician ever bestowed upon it, one which remains, to quote Wagner again, 'the model of supreme perfection in church music.'

An illustration of the manner in which his music has grown out of the liturgy is seen in the *Improperia* (or *Reproaches*) mentioned above, sung on Good Friday during the ceremony known as the Veneration of the Cross. No one who has ever been present on this occasion could fail to be profoundly impressed by the wonderful way in which the music is, as it were, a very part of the rite itself, to which it gives an unforgettable

3

impressiveness and spiritual beauty. And yet, looking at it in print, we feel it to be quite impossible that these few simple sustained chords and cadences (one may recall Berlioz's scornful description, technically correct, of course—'a few concords and suspensions') could produce such an overpowering effect, until it is realized that the music has been evolved out of the situation, instead of being composed for it, and that this very simplicity is the hall-mark of that genius which with unerring judgment found exactly the right musical utterance for the occasion.

Although Palestrina wrote some purely secular music, it does not in any way represent his creative powers at their highest; neither does it form any very considerable part of his work. It consists of ninety odd madrigals (many of them very short) and a few instrumental *ricercari* (of doubtful authenticity) which are sometimes played as string quartets, but are more probably organ pieces.

Against these we may set the great bulk of his work: 94 masses, nearly 500 motets, a number of other works in that style, and many smaller pieces, all of a liturgical or semi-liturgical character. We shall be justified, therefore, in thinking of him almost entirely as a composer of religious music, which is what he himself would certainly have wished, as is evident from a perusal of his own words on the subject in the celebrated preface to the fourth book of motets (settings of the *Song of Songs*), published in 1584 and dedicated to Gregory XIII, where he says:

There exists a vast mass of love-songs of the poets, written in a way that is entirely foreign to the profession and the name of Christian. They are the songs of men ruled by passion, and a great number of musicians, corrupters of youth, make them the concern of their art and their industry: and in proportion as they flourish by praise of their skill, so do they offend good and serious-minded men by the depraved taste of their work. I blush and grieve to think that once I was of their number. But since I cannot change the past, nor undo what is done, I have mended my ways. Therefore I have already laboured on those songs which have been written in praise of Our Lord Jesus Christ, and His most Holy Virgin-Mother Mary; and now I have produced a work which treats of the divine love of Christ and His Spouse the Soul, the Canticle of Solomon.

Even in earlier years he had said something to the same effect, although in less emphatic language. In the preface to the book of motets issued in 1569, he speaks of 'those who devote their gifts to light and vain ideas' and declares that for his part, now that he had attained maturity and was almost elderly [1] ('matura jam et vergenti ad senium aetate'),

whatever gifts I possess, although they may be of little account, will in future always be devoted to something more dignified and serious, worthy of a Christian being.

By some commentators all this has been characterized as the most blatant hypocrisy, dictated by the desire to curry favour with the Holy See, especially as, two years later, he published another book of secular madrigals, although these had been composed much earlier. But making allowances for a certain exaggeration and for the fact that Palestrina was still, at this time (1584), hoping for the much-coveted post as director of the Papal Choir (a wish that was never to be fulfilled), one may reasonably read into his words a realization on his part that his genius was almost wholly and essentially that of a church musician. [2] On this account he is, in some respects, a unique figure, for he is the only one of the great masters whose fame rests entirely upon religious music. It is true that the *Missa solemnis* alone would have assured Beethoven his place

---

[1] He was only about forty-four years of age at this time.
[2] See Berlioz's remarks quoted on p. 165.

among the immortals, but equally so would the symphonies or
the quartets or the pianoforte sonatas. One may say the same
about Bach and his religious and secular works. But Palestrina's secular madrigals would merely have placed him among
the lesser lights of his day, such as Marenzio. Judged by
his masses and motets he stands by the side of Bach and
Beethoven.

Yet the very splendour and greatness of his work has taken
it outside the realm of church music into that wider field where
both religious and secular music are to be regarded purely as
artistic manifestations. It is true that, as already stated, it will
be best understood and appreciated when associated with the
high purpose for which it was intended, but that is no reason
why there should not be secular performances of his works.
A piece of medieval glass displays its beauty most fully when
set in the stone mullions of a cathedral window, but its colour
and design can still be admired in the prosaic surroundings of
a sale-room.

Although Palestrina's music could never be popular in the
accepted sense of the word, it would probably enjoy a wider
appreciation among the more cultured musical public if opportunities of hearing some of the best works occurred more often.
Their religious nature should be no bar to an oratorio-loving
public; but a disadvantage from the practical standpoint,
tending to keep them outside the ordinary choral repertory of
the concert room, is the fact that the music is sung without any
instrumental addition of orchestra or organ and contains no
solo movements.

Nevertheless there is no reason why some of the masses should
not be given a place in the programmes of festivals and other
important musical functions. A few of the motets, and a
madrigal or so, do indeed occasionally find their way into
choral concerts of the more aesthetic type, but the great majority

of the finest works have never been heard here at all, and our musical life is the poorer for this neglect.

Those two modern channels for musical propaganda, the gramophone and the wireless, have done but little to help in spreading any knowledge or foster any appreciation of Palestrina's music. Only a very few records are available, and as far as our own radio programmes are concerned it is a rare occurrence for anything by the composer to figure therein. Other European stations, however, are a little less neglectful of this beautiful art of a bygone age.

Palestrina employs a musical diction which must seem somewhat strange and unfamiliar to those who are acquainted mostly with the music of the eighteenth, nineteenth and twentieth centuries, and the mistake is often made of regarding this sixteenth-century music of Palestrina and his contemporaries as in some respects crude and elementary compared with modern musical art. But in point of fact it is just as highly organized a system as any of our styles of musical composition to-day, and it will also be realized that Palestrina's music has as profound a humanity as that of Bach or Beethoven, and is as vital a manifestation of musical art as theirs.

It is true that the work of every great creative artist is to a certain extent the summing-up of an epoch. In the scheme of musical history Palestrina must be placed amongst those whose work it was thus to fructify and bring to its greatest perfection some already established form. Just as the symphony of Haydn and Mozart was developed by Beethoven and the music-drama of Monteverdi, Gluck and Weber by Wagner, so did ecclesiastical polyphonic music culminate with Palestrina.

For centuries before his day men had striven to enrich the plainsong, to adorn it in the service of the liturgy: at first crudely adding voices singing in octaves, fourths or fifths above

7

or below the melody, then venturing into simple new melodies, which could be combined with the original one, making an effect more or less pleasing to the ear. Here was the beginning of that method defined as counterpoint (*punctum contra punctum*), each note of one melody matched against each note of another. By the dawn of the sixteenth century these experiments had already produced remarkable work in the English, French and Netherlandish schools. The contrapuntal apparatus, the art of combining several melodies to sound simultaneously with good effect, had now reached a point at which there was only required a master-hand to perfect it, to make out of this almost mathematically strict counterpoint a living art, capable of producing music of the greatest beauty, a means by which, from fragments of plainsong or melodies from other sources, were spun threads of tone woven together into that tissue of sound known as polyphony.

Within this system Palestrina created a wonderful array of works—in a profusion hardly equalled by any other great composer—the majority of which, after a lapse of nearly four centuries, still compel our admiration because of their beauty, artistic sincerity and supreme musical craftsmanship. The very splendour of his achievement helped to make it a final flowering of the polyphonic art. There was no musician of Palestrina's calibre to succeed him in the field: even if there had been, it would have been almost impossible to develop any farther in the same direction, for two reasons. The first of these may be termed an internal one, since its explanation is to be found in Palestrina's music itself. At the beginning of the second half of the sixteenth century the French and Flemish polyphonic schools, especially the latter, were already beginning to show signs of developing along certain lines—especially in mannerisms of elaboration and over-ornamentation—tending towards a certain atmosphere (which for want of a better word may be termed secular) somewhat removed from the plainsong element whence the liturgical polyphonic form had evolved. Palestrina, from the time of writing the *Missa Papae Marcelli*, deflected the style back again to its origin, not only reverting to plainsong for his thematic ideas, in most cases, but also developing his contrapuntal melodies in a style that was as closely allied as possible to the plainsong melodies themselves, and often even suggesting their rhythms and contours. Within this limitation he created for his work a melodic style of a subtle and intimate character, quite distinct from that of other schools. Thus the roots of his art go down, through the polyphonic strata, deep into the subsoil of plainsong. It has been said, and with some truth, that the latter is in itself a complete art-form, incapable of any development in a musical sense. But if we could admit any such development, then the best of Palestrina's church music would undoubtedly represent it.

The second reason is an external one. If Palestrina had lived another ten years he would have witnessed the new experiments in harmony of Monteverdi and others, and in ten years more he would even have heard Frescobaldi's chromatic toccatas and fugues played by their composer in St Peter's itself during services. There is no reason to suppose that he was ignorant of this movement towards a new harmonic freedom, gained by the use of dissonance and the chromatic interval. In those madrigals which represent his excursion into the secular field —and for which, as we have seen, he apologized publicly in that address to Pope Gregory XIII—there are signs of experiments in the new ideas. But he deliberately turned his back upon them so far as his church music was concerned. Professor Jeppesen, in his study of the composer's musical style, speaks of him as having 'an almost antique sense of limitation' in this matter. But this limitation was deliberate, and the reason for Palestrina's attitude towards the newer style which was beginning to evolve is quite clear—a realization that the older, simpler system, within the ecclesiastical modes, was the better and more fitting for liturgical purposes.

At first sight it might seem merely a curious accident of history that a single half-century—roughly speaking the latter part of the sixteenth—produced for the services of the Catholic church music the aesthetic and liturgical perfection of which has never since been surpassed, or even equalled. This golden age of ecclesiastical music (as it has been termed), with Palestrina as its greatest figure and his contemporaries Orlande de Lassus and Victoria of the next importance, remains for that church an ideal. But from what has already been said it is clear that this apparently accidental circumstance was in reality the outcome of a combination of events. Towards the end of the sixteenth century great forces were swiftly at work. Secular music, which in the past had been nurtured almost entirely in the fold of the church—had used its modes (or scales), its notation, its rhythms and accents—now left that fold, made its own modes (the beginnings of our modern diatonic major and minor) and its own technique of composition, which included a new freedom in the use and treatment of dissonances. And it took ecclesiastical music with it into this new field. One has only to compare a mass written about 1650 with one of the older school to realize what had come about —a complete change of style and outlook. A few composers had continued to work for a time in the older manner, but the new forces were too powerful. By 1700 church music was definitely secularized, in that it was using the new idiom.

So potent was the influence of the latter that the music of the polyphonic period began to be neglected in the churches. What was happening in music was also manifested in other spheres of ecclesiastical art. If it were deemed an 'improvement' for the Gothic lines of a church to be hidden by baroque ornaments, one cannot be surprised that the impersonal mystic beauty of the music of the Palestrinian era should be considered uncouth, inexpressive and lacking in human qualities.[1] Hardly anywhere, save in Rome, did it continue in use.

The so-called 'reform of church music' in the sixteenth century, with which Palestrina's name has been associated, may be briefly discussed here. The earlier biographers, following the lead of Baini (1828), were wont to chronicle a dramatic moment in Palestrina's life: how, when music—other than plainsong—was in danger of complete banishment from the church by decree of the Council of Trent, the composer came forward with three masses, specially written to show a new, dignified and suitable style for liturgical use; how one of these, the famous *Missa Papae Marcelli*, was accepted by a committee of cardinals as fulfilling all their requirements, the said mass being then solemnly sung before the pope and approved by him also.

Recent research has shown that there is no foundation of fact to the story as it stands. The whole situation at this time, in the matter of church music, has been much exaggerated. It seems probable that the real position somewhat resembled one which, three and a half centuries later, called forth the *Motu proprio* of Pius X. In each case there were certain abuses. There was the secular element, this taking the form, in Palestrina's day, of the use of melodies derived from popular songs

[1] So soon after Palestrina's death did a new point of view prevail that even his pupil Anerio apparently thought to 'improve' his master's work by adding an instrumental *continuo* to several masses, among them the *Papae Marcelli*, reducing the latter to four parts! This was in 1619, but even earlier, in 1610, one Alessandro Nuvolini had made similar additions to other Palestrinian masses. In 1613 the *Song of Songs* was published with a *bassus ad organum* and the hymns were also similarly treated.

associated with unedifying words, and there may have been some truth in the assertion that the original words belonging to the tune were occasionally surreptitiously sung in church. Another point was the employment of too much musical elaboration, a third the confusion of the text by undesirable repetitions and interpolation. Palestrina's earlier work, by the way, was not entirely free from some of these defects.

These were not unreasonable criticisms. After all, one could scarcely expect the church authorities to regard with favour a mass founded upon a melody associated with Boccaccio, to quote one instance only. The necessity for some reform had been discussed from time to time and Pope Marcellus II, whose name is associated with Palestrina's celebrated mass, had already, in the few weeks of his brief reign, taken up the matter, which also claimed the attention of other 'reforming' pontiffs. But there is no evidence at all to support the statement that any of the popes either desired or intended to banish all music from the services of the church. Indeed, all that seems to have actually happened was that two of the commission of eight cardinals entrusted with carrying out the various recommendations of the Tridentine Council—among them that the church must 'exclude all music tainted with sensual and impure elements, all secular forms and unedifying language'[1]—sent for some of the papal singers. The latter were asked to perform several masses (or movements) from their repertory, chiefly with a view to ascertaining whether the liturgical text was obscured or improperly added to. We do

[1] The actual words of the recommendation, in the Tridentine session of 17th September 1562, were: 'Ab ecclesiis vero musicas eas, ubi sive organo, sive cantu lascivum aut impurum aliquid miscetur, item saeculares omnes actiones, vana atque adeo profana colloquia, arceant ut domus Dei vere domus orationis esse videatur ac dici possit.'

not even know if any of Palestrina's music was sung on this occasion, but it is quite possible, since one of the papal choir-books at that time contained three of his masses.

Apparently the cardinals were satisfied with what they heard; for nothing more seems to have been done in the matter, an interesting reference to which is to be found in a book published in 1629 by the Jesuit priest Fr di Cressoli, in which he states that the fathers of his society in Rome told him how Pius IV had withdrawn his opposition to church music because of Palestrina's masses: they made this statement, says this writer, having heard it from the composer himself. Fr di Cressoli also asserts that the pope was induced to listen to several masses specially written by Palestrina to prove that the sacred texts could be suitably treated. Here we probably have the source from which Baini's imaginative story was evolved.

CHAPTER II

THE PERSONAL PICTURE

i. The Man

THE known facts concerning Palestrina's life are not extensive, but they are sufficient; especially those brought to light by recent research to enable us to form a certain picture of the composer and his activities. A recent writer[1] has described him as 'a modest, peaceable and kindly Italian citizen,' and in some respects this rather conventional estimate of him may be true. A sober-minded man, of irreproachable moral character and sound piety, a kind husband and father, generous to all his kinsfolk, in his relations with the external world he seems to have commanded personal respect as well as admiration for his genius. Although doubtless aware of his own commanding gifts, he was apparently free from that petty jealousy of other musicians which has so often beset even the greatest artists.

An instance of his admiration for the music of his contemporaries is furnished by the records of the Julian Choir (of St Peter's), in which, under date of December 1589, is to be found an entry relating to payment for copies made, by Palestrina's order, of works by Morales. And a proof of the esteem in which they in turn held him is to be found in the remarkable tribute of affection paid to him in the latter years of his life, an account of which will be found elsewhere in this book.

But there is another, less conventional, aspect of his character. It is difficult to imagine the creator of the *Missa Papae Marcelli*

[1] Knud Jeppesen, in *The Style of Palestrina and the Dissonance*.

14

engaged in producing wine and selling it by the barrel; building and buying house property and letting it out; or to think of him as devoting one part of his day to the somewhat dingy business of a furrier's shop and the other part to writing music of such rare beauty as the *Missa Assumpta est*; or descending, when in the full maturity of his genius, to a pretence of valuing the musical judgment of a second-rate amateur (Duke Guglielmo Gonzaga) sufficiently to declare that he would have liked to submit to the latter, for 'suggestions and corrections,' a collection of motets before publishing them. Yet he did these things.

Modesty may have been one of his attributes, but sometimes he practised the virtue with an ostentation that makes one inclined to suspect its sincerity: another instance may be given, from the preface to the 1575 book of motets, where he declares he only consented to publish them at the entreaty of his friends ('amicorum rogatu in lucem edere decrevissem').[1] The truth is he was both modest and proud; the legitimate belief in his gifts which, like every other great composer, he had is evident, for in more than one of these prefaces he says something like this: 'Others may think I am not without talent, yet I myself know how little it is,' etc.

There seems to have been something commercial and opportunist on the one hand, something spiritual and mystic on the other, in the make-up of his personality. The second of these factors made his art largely what it is and the first was probably not unbeneficial. His life, indeed, was not without that inconsistency so often associated with the artistic

[1] This preface ends up with a fanciful touch on Palestrina's part. He begs the Duke of Ferrara (to whom the motets are dedicated) to accept them in the same spirit as the great Artaxerxes once accepted a cup of cold water offered by a peasant. Those who have read Cecil Gray's recent biography of Sibelius will notice that the latter also uses the same simile, in speaking of his own music.

temperament. Thus he could at one moment aspire to the priesthood (soon after his first wife's death), and actually enter the clerical state, only to turn from his high purpose a few weeks later, after meeting with a well-to-do young widow, whom he married forthwith.

It was, of course, quite natural for him to marry again, especially as, like Bach, he had found in a peaceful domesticity exactly the congenial atmosphere for his creative work. But the circumstance of this and many other incidents in his life seem again to point to a nature spiritual on the one hand, worldly on the other.[1] The latter trait was no doubt an inheritance from that race of small landowners from which he was descended. From them he evidently inherited also that independence of spirit which seems to have been a strongly marked characteristic. He was not afraid to 'walk out,' in the literal sense of the words, of St John Lateran, leaving his post at a moment's notice—a bold proceeding in those times, for a mere musician—when annoyed at new financial regulations introduced by the chapter. When his patron the Duke of Mantua sent compositions by himself for Palestrina's approval the latter was quite candid about the shortcomings of the noble amateur's music. He even dared to grumble publicly to Pope Sixtus V in the dedicatory preface (appropriately enough!) to his setting of the *Lamentations*, about what he considered the inadequate reward his art had brought him.

[1] The dual nature of his personality seems again apparent in such things as his dealings with patrons like Duke Guglielmo Gonzaga. Tempted by the idea that princely music-lovers so anxious to secure his services would pay a high price for them, Palestrina asked large sums. Yet the thought that his spiritual home was in Rome, and the knowledge that he might lose the atmosphere and the opportunity for creative work, made him fix the price at a figure he knew the patron would not be likely to accept.

Palestrina liked money; he was fond of dabbling in property, buying and selling houses—at one time he possessed four, which he let out—vineyards and fields from time to time. The picture of him as a pathetic poverty-stricken figure, which Baini, in his biography, has imagined, does not fit in with the facts. He was not badly off at any time in his career, for he always endeavoured, quite justifiably, of course, to obtain the best possible price for his services and displayed much shrewd-ness in bargaining. Doubtless those popes and cardinals who accorded him their patronage considered that he did very well, for a mere musician.

In view of the difficulty of comparing money values of the sixteenth century with those of to-day, and the differing stan-dards of life, it is not possible to estimate Palestrina's financial position exactly, but it seems to have been comparable to that of the average cathedral organist in England to-day. He seems to have spent money freely and not to have saved much, for when the dowry his son Rodolfo had received with his wife had to be repaid, after Rodolfo's death, Palestrina was obliged to raise the money by a loan, on interest. Probably a part of what he acquired went to relatives, and apparently he spent a good deal on publishing his own works.

Music printing was costly: the setting up had to be done by innumerable tiny wood-blocks, a slow and laborious process, and paper was dear. Title pages were often engraved most elaborately, with pictures and decorative patterns, dedicatory prefaces being set out in special type, while each page of music was usually adorned with one or more fine woodcuts.[1] The

[1] The early editions in the British Museum are worth inspection as artistic productions, apart from their musical contents. Thus the 1567 book of masses has beautifully engraved pictures of the Saviour, the Blessed Virgin (see plate facing p. 126), the saints and other re-ligious subjects, while now and again a few *amorini* and portraits of

large folio editions must have been very expensive productions and even the smaller books contain many of the same decorative touches. Not much of this outlay could be covered by such sales as the music enjoyed. Choirs were small numerically, and in the case of the larger books their big music type allowed two or three singers to share the same book, the different parts being often printed opposite each other to suit this arrangement. Furthermore there was no copyright law, as we know it to-day, in existence at that time. Any protection operated only over a limited area, outside which music was freely copied; even 'pirated' editions were produced, while foreign countries invariably appropriated music without any payment to the composer.

Also he seems to have maintained a more pretentious establishment than the average musician of his day, for we know that he kept at least two servants at one time.

All these facts must be borne in mind when we read the remarkable outburst on the subject of his finances addressed to Pope Sixtus V, in the preface referred to on a previous page. In it he says:

Worldly cares of any kind, Most Holy Father, are adverse to the Muses, and particularly those which arise from a lack of private means. For when the latter afford a sufficiency (and to ask more is the mark of a greedy and intemperate man) the mind can more easily detach itself from other cares—if not, the fault lies within. Those who have experienced the necessity of labouring to provide this sufficiency, according to their rank and way of life, know full well how it distracts the mind from learning, and from a study of the liberal arts.

I have certainly known this experience all my lifetime, and

gallants have, somewhat incongruously, strayed into the pages. Another book, of motets (1573), shows exquisite little views, apparently of contemporary Rome—churches, villas, piazzas, etc.

THE COMPOSER'S STATUE IN HIS NATIVE CITY

*This was erected in the central piazza of Palestrina by the city fathers
in 1921. The inscription reads: 'A Giovanni Pierluigi, Principe della
Musica'*

especially at present. But I thank the Divine Goodness, first that now the course is almost finished, and the goal in sight: secondly that in the midst of the greatest difficulties, I have never interrupted my study of music: for what other interest could I have had, as a man dedicated to the profession from boyhood, and engrossed in it to the best of my ability and energies? (Would that my progress had equalled my labour and diligence!)

I have composed and published much: a great deal more is lying by me, which I am hindered from publishing because of the straitened means of which I have spoken. It would need no little expenditure, especially if the larger notes and letters are used, which church publications really require.

Meanwhile, I have only been able to publish, in this smaller format, those Lamentations of the Prophet Jeremiah which are usually sung in choral form during Holy Week in the churches.

This work I offer to your Holiness with that humility due to the exalted Pastor of the Universal Catholic Church, outstanding in holiness and admirable in authority.

At the date when this appeared in print (1588) Palestrina was about sixty-three years of age and had not only known sorrow, but felt some dissatisfaction with his musical career. The note of bitterness which underlies his plaint may have been partly due to the realization that one honour he coveted above all others—the rank of Master of the Papal Choir— could never be his, for Pope Sixtus had decreed that the appointment must go to the members of the choir in order of seniority. Palestrina, as only a pensioned-off member, and holding the somewhat indefinite post of 'composer to the choir,' was therefore ineligible.

But perhaps the chief reason, as the composer himself says, was a certain disappointment in seeing so much of his work still in manuscript and a realization that to attempt to publish it all would mean an expense for which he had not the money. At the time (1588) there had been published four books of masses (twenty-seven works), seven books of motets (over 200 pieces) and three collections of madrigals, probably representing together a good deal less than half of his creative work up to the date mentioned. At the time of Palestrina's death (2nd February 1594) six more volumes had been added to these, but, even so, some of his greatest masterpieces remained unpublished.

On a preceding page a certain parallel was drawn between the lives of Palestrina and Bach—their love of domesticity. The comparison might be extended, first in the matter of creative activity: Palestrina's profusion of masses and motets is matched by Bach's outpouring of church cantatas, motets and chorale preludes; the Roman composer had three sons, who, like some of Bach's, inherited much of their father's musical gifts and were personally trained by him to be excellent musicians; and the manner in which Iginio, Palestrina's only surviving son, endeavoured after his father's death to exploit any musical material left unpublished or unfinished by the composer also reminds us of similar action by Bach's sons.

ii. The Musician

It is probable that Palestrina's artistic gifts were derived from the maternal side, for there was a certain Veccia (this was his mother's maiden name) occupying the post of organist at St Agapit's Cathedral in the town of Palestrina during the latter part of the composer's life, who was evidently a relative. And there is the fact that two of his brothers, Bernardino and Silla, were both musical, especially the latter. On the other hand, there is no record of any musical ability existing on his father's side.

Of his personality as a musician we know but little, except what his music can tell us. A study of it makes one realize that no composer was ever surer of himself than Palestrina. He seems always to have known exactly what he wanted to do, and how to do it; so that his music always gives one the impression of being logical and controlled. There are, however, interesting glimpses of his views to be found in the few letters of his that have survived and also in those prefaces to the books of masses and motets issued by him, to which reference has already been made. Beethoven's famous saying about finding a 'new road' to take in music is recalled by Palestrina's expressed determination, in the dedicatory preface to his first book of masses, 'to sing the praises of God in a finer manner [*exquisitioribus rhythmis*].' This is reiterated with even more emphasis in the preface to the second book of masses, twelve years later, in which Palestrina says: 'I have essayed to adorn the Holy Sacrifice of the Mass with music written in a new style [*novo modorum*] and in accordance with the views of the most serious and religiousminded persons in high places.'

The assertion of a new style was amply justified in view of the fact that this particular collection of masses included the *Papae Marcelli*, a work which in many ways constituted a departure from the older methods of Palestrina's predecessors, and indeed from his own early work. His sense of style, too, is evident from the preface to the settings of the Song of Solomon, wherein he says, speaking of the actual music: 'I have used a style rather more spirited [*genere aliquantum alacriore*] than I am wont to employ in church [i.e. liturgical] compositions, for so I consider the subject to demand this treatment.'

Palestrina, in spite of his tremendous output, seems often to have worked slowly and to have spent much time in revision. This is borne out by his own statement in the dedicatory address of the book of motets, offered to Cardinal Carpi, in which he speaks of the musical contents as having been in preparation for some years previously, 'composed with continuous application and, so far as in me lies, polished with such art as I possess.'

Again and again he insists on this aspect of his work, the time and the care spent on polishing and perfecting the music. With Palestrina this evidently counted for almost as much as the ideas themselves. As far as the latter were concerned he was governed by two principles—the one laid down by himself in a letter to the Duke of Mantua—'dare spirito vivo alle parole' ('giving a living spirit to the words') and the maxim enunciated by Pope Marcellus II that what was sung should 'be heard and understood' (*audiri percipique*).

In the preface just mentioned Palestrina also has a few homely, common-sense words to say about church music which are as true to-day as they were nearly 400 years ago:

Our wisest mortals have decided that it [music] should give a zest to divine worship, so that those whom pious devotion to religious practices has led to the temple might remain there delighting in voices blending in harmony.

If men take such pains to compose beautiful music for profane songs, one should at least devote as much thought to sacred song, nay, even more than to mere worldly matters.

Therefore, though well aware of my feeble powers, I have held nothing more desirable than that whatever is sung throughout the year, according to the season, should be acceptable to the ear by its vocal beauty so far as it lay in my power to make it so.

Very little of Palestrina's correspondence (if indeed he indulged much in letter-writing) has been preserved, but there exist some records of letters which passed between him and Duke Guglielmo Gonzaga, in which we get a glimpse of his views of composition. The correspondence deals with works commissioned by the duke, with music composed by him and sent to Palestrina for criticism. He was evidently of a very practical disposition where such matters were concerned, his commercial instincts blending admirably with a sound artistic judgment. Also he was at all times ready and willing to write to order. The duke commissions a mass to be sung in the new church of St Barbara he had recently erected in Mantua. Palestrina, in sending the work, points out that he did not know whether it was to be a short or a long one, in simple or more elaborate style, and if the clarity of text was to be a first consideration. If the mass he had composed, therefore, was not suitable, might he be allowed to write another?

The duke selects texts for some motets he wishes Palestrina to compose. In sending them back the latter is anxious to point out that possibly the music *may* not be quite up to his usual standard, as he has been ill. ('I spent many days in bed,' he says.) The duke inquires about the celebrated *faux-bourdons* sung by the Papal Choir during Holy Week; Palestrina replies that they do not exist in writing, but he will put them on paper; and he will also like the duke to see a few he himself has written, adding: 'These are just trifles, in three parts only; they may be meaningless, but they sound well.'

He writes to the duke quite candidly about the deficiencies of the latter's music. After a few conventional words of praise for the refined style of a motet he continues:

I have marked a few places where the harmony would be clearer with fewer notes, there at the sixth and the unison, where the parts go up and down, and again at the sixth and fifth, and similarly some unisons in the fugue seem to give a forced movement to the parts—and at the *stretto* the words may be obscured, a fault to be found in second-rate work.

Some years later, when the duke forwarded a mass for criticism, Palestrina seems to have hesitated over sending a reply, probably because he felt his opinion was bound to be unfavourable; he therefore asked a mutual friend to write and

explain the delay on the ground of being busily engaged in composing music for the *Lamentations*, at Pope Gregory's request.
When he was at length obliged to return the manuscript,
his criticism was quite frank; in addition to marking a number
of places where he thought improvements could be made, he
said: 'I have not touched the *Pleni sunt coeli*, because I think
that if you have the leisure you might perhaps like to rewrite it!'

There may have been more of these 'postal correspondence
lessons': we know that a madrigal was also sent by the duke,
but Palestrina's criticism and corrections of this have apparently
not been preserved.[1] He also seems to have been an excellent
teacher: some of his pupils, such as Zoilo, Marenzio and
Anerio, achieved considerable reputations.

Two interesting facts about his methods of working at
composition emerge from this correspondence. One is that
he was in the habit of trying over passages on the lute as he
proceeded with a work, just as, in later times, composers have,
in the same way, used the pianoforte. Then, in one letter to
the duke, apropos of the motet by the latter which had been
sent to him for criticism, he says that he has made a score
(apparently the music existed only in the separate parts,
according to the custom of the day) in order to judge the
effects better. So there can be little doubt that his own
compositions were worked out in detail by means of a full
score.

We get a further glimpse of the practical musician at work
when, in 1578, the duke asked for a set of masses [2] on certain

[1] The duke evidently took the criticisms in good part, for the
friendship continued until his death.

[2] The masses have not been identified; they may never have been
published. It is probable that they were very simple compositions,
in three or four parts only. One may infer this from two facts:
Palestrina wrote them (seven in all) in a few months and the choir

plainchant themes selected by himself. Palestrina's sense of tonality was evidently very keen: we find him explaining to the duke that one of these *canti fermi* will have to be transposed, as it had apparently been written in a mode (the fourth) to which, in the composer's opinion, it did not really belong. He mentions that the second one (the duke sent him two only at first) is in the proper (authentic) mode and therefore need not be altered.

---

at Mantua could not tackle anything very difficult or elaborate, judging by the music of the two motets for St Barbara's feast which Palestrina had previously written for these ducal singers.

CHAPTER III

ANCESTORS—EARLY DAYS

IT is nowadays a biographical fashion to inquire into the racial origin of the subject. In the case of Palestrina this is perhaps not a very difficult task. It is quite possible that he was directly descended from some Roman citizen of classical days—a soldier or a farmer. His features, as shown in the various existing portraits, are of a type resembling those of many busts of old Romans to be seen in museums and galleries.

The earliest known portrait is that which appears on the engraved frontispiece of the first book of masses, when Palestrina would be between thirty and thirty-one. It shows him apparently full of vitality, with a face of much animation, a luxuriant head of hair and a full beard. The later portraits, those in the Vatican and the oratory of St Philip Neri at Rome, done when he was in the early fifties, are remarkable for their grave, almost stern, expression and ascetic, careworn features.

These portraits all suggest a striking personal appearance and a fine physique, although we know that he suffered a good deal from illness. This, however, is scarcely surprising when it is remembered how Rome and the papal kingdom generally were continually afflicted with war, famine and pestilence, and one must be thankful that he escaped the epidemics which carried off his first wife, two sons and a brother, and that he was spared long enough to complete his creative work.

It is quite certain that his forbears had lived for centuries in or near his birthplace, Palestrina, the small city of the Papal States the name of which, at first only added to that of his own

—Giovanni Pierluigi [1]—was in the end entirely substituted for the latter. From earliest days Palestrina — or Praeneste, as it was known in classical times—had been closely connected with Rome, only twenty-five miles distant, the ancient *Via Praenestina* running direct from the imperial city.

Giovanni Pierluigi's ancestors were worthy folk, small land-owners possessing one or two houses and vineyards, a hard-working race, honest and also pious, for many of their names have been discovered in the records of the confraternity of Corpus Christi belonging to the neighbourhood. The first definite records to be found of the composer's family do not, however, date back very far—to the middle of the fifteenth century, when his paternal grandfather Pierluisci, or Pierlouisco (as the name was then spelt), seems to have been born about 1450, his death taking place in 1522. In a legal document of 1510 he is referred to as *discretus vir*, thus confirming the good reputation of the family.

In the will of his widow Jacobella, a Palestrinian by birth, who died at Rome in 1527, there is a supposed reference to the composer, her property—a house in Palestrina, a little money and a considerable quantity of household goods—being divided among various relatives, including Sante Pierluigi, her son, and his wife Palma (the composer's parents), and also a certain 'Io, nepoti suo' (to quote the Latin text of the will). 'Io' would, of course, stand for Ioannes (Giovanni), but the

---

[1] The process had already begun during Palestrina's life: in his published works he describes himself as Joannes Petrus-Aloysius Praenestinus, the Latin form of Giovanni Pierluigi da Palestrina ('John Peter-Lewis of Palestrina'). In documents of the period his name appears in various ways, e.g. Joannes praenestinus, Giovanni da Penestrina (!), Gio Pietro Luigi da Pallestrina; and in some madrigal collections he is called Gianetto Palestina, or del Pelestino.

word 'nepoti' might be taken to mean either a grandson or a nephew. Since the composer was probably only about two years old, perhaps less, at this time, there is some doubt as to whether the reference is to him, particularly as the bequest consisted of a mattress and ten kitchen utensils. However, as the good lady left an unusual quantity of mattresses, pots and pans (Cametti thinks she may have kept a small inn at Rome), it is possible that these were meant to be sold and the money laid by for the infant Giovanni.

The house mentioned was one of two in the possession of Sante Pierluigi at the time of Palestrina's birth. We do not know on what date his father was born (probably at the end of the fifteenth century), nor when his marriage took place with Palma Veccia (also a Palestrinian), but if we accept the 'Io' of the will as meaning the composer, Sante Pierluigi was probably married about 1522.

Palma Pierluigi died in 1536, leaving three other sons besides Giovanni. Three or four years later her husband was married again to a certain Maria Gismondi, his death taking place in 1554, just after he had seen his gifted son installed as master of the choristers at the Julian Choir in St Peter's and already known as a composer of repute (his first volume of masses being published the same year).

Sante Pierluigi seems to have been an honest, pious, indus-trious and fairly well-to-do citizen. He possessed land in addition to two houses, one of which was demolished only in fairly recent times; the other, where he lived, and where the composer was born, is still standing, although probably to some extent rebuilt, for the city fathers of Palestrina have placed upon it the following inscription: 'Nel fabbricato interno di questa casa nacque ed abitò Giovanni Pierluigi, Principe della Musica' ('Within these walls Giovanni Pierluigi, Prince of Music, was born and lived'). The cautious phrase 'nel fab-

(4) He was a choirboy at Santa Maria Maggiore in 1537.

(5) A contemporary obituary notice gives his age at his death as sixty-eight.

(6) His mother died in 1536, leaving several children, of whom he was apparently the eldest.

(7) His first church appointment dates from 1544 and his marriage took place in 1547.

If (5) were correct (1) would seem a deliberate exaggeration, since at the earliest Palestrina could not have taken any active part in services—either as chorister or altar-boy—at an earlier age than about seven years. But it is quite possible that (5) is wrong and that Palestrina may have been sixty-nine or even seventy at his death.[1]

The veracity of (3) is very doubtful, for it has been discovered that this inscription dates only from the eighteenth century.

(2), which (6) also seems to support, would place his birth before 1527, and other evidence connected with (4) suggests that he was one of the elder choirboys, perhaps twelve or thirteen at the date mentioned. If so he would be nineteen or twenty on receiving his first appointment in 1544, which seems quite a reasonable assumption.

We know very little of his childhood days. But living only a stone's throw from the cathedral of St Agapit, one may be quite sure that the little Giovanni (or Gianetto as he was called) had his musical gifts first developed by the music of the services there, which were apparently on a high level. Much of the music that was performed in the Roman basilicas at this time would have found its way to St Agapit's—masses and motets by

---

[1] Such contemporary mistakes are not uncommon: even in our own time a case has occurred, for many of the biographical notices of Delius published during his lifetime gave the date of his birth incorrectly by one year.

Josquin des Prés, Pierre de la Rue, Okeghem, Dufay and others of the French and Flemish schools—and so his youthful ear was from earliest days familiar with the way in which the vocal strands of this early polyphonic music were woven together. No doubt as a child he would be occasionally taken to Rome, only twenty miles distant, for the family had relatives living there, and on these occasions there might have been visits to the basilicas, with the opportunity of hearing their choirs, even the Papal Choir itself. And there is every reason to believe that the little Pierluigi became a chorister of St Agapit's at an early age.

In 1534 the bishop of Palestrina (Cardinal Andrea della Valle) was made arch-priest of the basilica of Santa Maria Maggiore in Rome, and it is quite likely he took with him to his new church the little cathedral choirboy whose unusual musical intelligence had no doubt attracted attention, and entered him in the choir-school there. This, at any rate, is the most probable explanation of how he came to be in the basilican choir, a fact proved by an entry in the archives of the chapter showing him to have been a chorister there in 1537.

The choir-school was run on lines that have since become familiar elsewhere. A contract was made between the parents and the basilican chapter, the boys being lodged, clothed, fed and given a general education in return for their services in church. Sound, simple instruction which included Latin was provided for the ordinary school curriculum, and in addition to their vocal training the boys received a course of musical theory, including counterpoint. If a boy were withdrawn by his parents without the chapter's consent the cost of his keep from the date of entering the school had to be refunded.

So important a part did these *scholae cantorum* play in the music of their day that one biographer has remarked that the history of these Roman choirs was to some extent the history of the Roman school of sacred music at the most classic period of its existence.

The limits of age for entrance into the choir-school were from seven to ten years, and Palestrina may have been enrolled, as already suggested, in 1534, when he would have been nine or ten years of age. The exact date of his leaving the choir is not known, but it was probably early in 1540, when he would be between fifteen and sixteen. Apparently he went home for a short time, then returned to Rome in the same year, for in a contemporary chronicle written by a Palestrinian citizen we read that 'about 1540 one of our fellow-citizens, named Giovanni Pierluigi, went off to Rome to study music.'

Much has been written in an endeavour to settle the question of who is to be regarded as the composer's teacher during this period. While a choirboy he would have received a certain amount of musical tuition, as we have seen, from the choir-master in charge at Santa Maria Maggiore; this would be the French musician Robin Mallapert, who resigned the post in 1539: for the next few months the position was held by one Robert de Fevin, after which the appointment of Firmin Le Bel in 1540 is found in the archives. We may assume it was the last-named musician with whom Palestrina completed his studies on returning to Rome; and we shall probably not be far wrong in assuming that he made himself generally useful at the basilica, no doubt helping to teach the younger boys, copy music, etc., while perfecting his knowledge of counterpoint and composition generally. Also he learned to play the organ.

Palestrina remained in Rome until the autumn of 1544, when he obtained his first appointment—a post at the cathedral of his native city. He was nineteen or twenty years of age at the time when he signed the contract for his services with the

ST. AGAPIT'S CATHEDRAL

A glimpse of the west front of Palestrina's cathedral, where the composer held his first appointment. In front of the entrance door is an old fountain

both of the marriage settlement and the inheritance make amusing reading; we can hardly imagine the composer of the *Papae Marcelli* Mass as the proud possessor of an 'asinello di pelame color castano' ('chestnut-coloured donkey').

At any rate the young couple seem to have been comfortably off with Pierluigi's emoluments from the cathedral and his wife's portion. Two sons were born while they remained at Palestrina—Rodolfo in 1549 and Angelo in 1551, just before the composer left his native town once more for Rome.

Nothing more is known of this period of his life. We may be sure that he kept in touch with Rome and its music and that he was busy composing. Many of the compositions which subsequently appeared in print were no doubt written during those seven years, although probably subjected to revision later on. Even some of the works which were published during the latter part of his life possibly date from this time.

The *ricercari* for organ attributed to Palestrina, to which reference has already been made, if they are really his work, would probably belong to this period. A set of eight are printed in the Breitkopf & Härtel complete edition, and according to Grove (1st edition, vol. iii, 1883) the late Dr W. H. Cummings possessed a manuscript dating from the end of the sixteenth century, in which are twenty-two by 'Gianetto Palestina,' a corruption of the composer's name which occurs elsewhere in connection with his early period. These latter, as far as one is aware, have never been published.

What kind of an organ he played on at St Agapit's we do not know. In the basilica of St John Lateran at Rome there is still preserved a small portable organ of the *positif* type, dating from the time when the composer himself was choirmaster at that church (from 1555 to 1560). It is a one-manual instrument without any pedals, of course. For the benefit of those readers who may be organists the specification is here given: Bourdon, 8 ft.; Montre, 4 ft.; Nazard, 3 ft.; Octave, 2 ft.; Larigot, 1⅓ ft. and Piccolo, 1 ft. Doubtless such an organ was carried to various chapels in the basilica to accompany singers, and was therefore a choir organ in the literal sense of the term. There may have been a similar instrument at St Agapit's, but in all probability the cathedral possessed in addition a larger organ, which was the one the composer would play at festivals, according to his contract. It was evidently an instrument of some importance, since (according to Raugel) there is a record of its renovation at the expense of a citizen, Baldovino Veccia, about 1570. The latter was the father of the young musician Giovanni Veccia, already mentioned, who, after studying with Palestrina, became organist at St Agapit's a little later. Probably these Veccias were kinsfolk of his mother, Palma Veccia.

CHAPTER IV

THE RETURN TO ROME

THE election of Cardinal del Monte as pope in 1551 was an event of great importance to the young musician. A few months after he began his reign Julius III sent for the brilliant organist-composer attached to his former see and made him master of the Julian Choir belonging to St Peter's. It was a tremendous stroke of good fortune for Palestrina. At the age of about twenty-six he thus occupied a position of the first importance and stood on the threshold of a brilliant career in the musical world of Rome.

As he took up his new duties he must have been inspired by the sight of the massive walls of the new St Peter's which were beginning to rise around the ancient basilica of Constantine. And the city itself was undergoing some transformation, with new palaces and villas springing up in many places. But the future was to bring disappointments and disillusions such as have always beset the path of the creative artist. Nevertheless Palestrina was never the pathetic, poverty-stricken figure the earlier biographers loved to represent. Neither did he ever endure such humiliations as were suffered by other great composers—for instance, Bach, who had as a young man to wear the livery of a *heyduck*, and Mozart, obliged to sit down to dinner with cooks and valets. Palestrina, thanks to a little patrimony and his wife's inheritance, was always able to preserve a certain ndependence.

The Julian Choir, of which he was now the head, was so called after its founder, Julius II, who had instituted it for the services of the basilica in 1513. When Palestrina came to take charge the choir had already established a fine tradition through musicians such as Arcadelt, Domenico Ferrabosco and Francesco Roussel.

Palestrina's immediate predecessor was Robin Mallapert, who apparently vacated the post in his favour, whether willingly or not we do not know. As soon as Palestrina assumed office he was given the full control of the choir. His predecessor had only been styled *magister chori*, whereas he was known as *maestro di cappella*. His salary was six scudi[1] a month, with other (varying) emoluments. The choir at this time was a small, select body of well-paid singers—three male sopranos (two of whom seem to have been his pupils), three altos, three tenors and three basses appear to have been all that it mustered when Palestrina assumed control. He seems to have procured his brother Bernardino some sort of post in the choir, probably as librarian or music copyist, or both, for in 1554 the archives record that one 'Belardino' who styled himself 'brother to Messer Giovanni Pierluigi' bought for the use of the Julian Choir a set of the part-books of his brother's first book of masses and also arranged for them to be suitably bound.

The musical repertory of the choir at the time of Palestrina's appointment probably consisted almost entirely of works by the popular French and Flemish composers, with perhaps one or two works by such an Italian as Costanzo Festa; but the new choirmaster was perhaps able to include some of his own. Soon after settling down he was hard at work composing—a new mass in honour of his august patron, and a revision of some earlier ones, destined to be printed and offered by dedication to Pope Julius.

[1] The scudo, so named from the shield on its face, was the equivalent of the medieval crown. Its actual value in terms of our own money to-day cannot, of course, be estimated.

This task occupied him almost three years. In spite of his enormous output Palestrina seems to have composed slowly and always subjected his work to careful revision (as he him-self says, in the preface quoted in an earlier chapter), although Cametti declares (on what evidence he does not say) that at the height of his powers the composer's facility was so remark-able that he could write a mass in ten days. It is significant that in one of the few instances that Palestrina apparently wrote a work in a hurry, the result failed to please the reigning pontiff, who showed himself an excellent critic in declaring that the music in question, the Mass *Tu es pastor ovium*, was not up to the composer's standard, comparing it with the *Papae Marcelli* to the disadvantage of the former. It must be remem-bered that he was writing music continuously for nearly fifty years: even so, unless he was a very quick worker, only by immense industry and application could he have achieved so much.

At first sight it might seem surprising that nothing of his had appeared in print up to this date. But one must remember the times. Music printing and publishing were still more or less in their infancy and also costly: even important works remained in manuscript, and usually not in full score. Especially was this the case with religious music, which existed mostly in part-books, copied and taken to other churches from time to time. Thus the issue of this first volume in 1554, printed by the famous Dorici brothers of Rome (at the composer's expense, of course), was something of an event in his life. Seven copies of this historic publication are still in existence, five of them in Italy. It was artistically produced—an elaborate title-page, all engraved, in the centre the pope seated, wearing the triple tiara, in the act of receiving the open volume from the com-poser, who, on bended knee and wearing the cassock and sur-plice of a choirmaster, is receiving the papal blessing. Inside, the volume contained equally flattering homage, for the first mass was entitled *Ecce sacerdos magnus*, its *canto fermo* being the plainsong theme of the vespers antiphon for the commemoration of a pontiff-confessor. So that there should be no mistake as to who was meant, the printer placed a tiny woodcut of Julius III's coat-of-arms against the *canto fermo* every time it appeared in each part. Even the singers were not allowed to forget in whose honour the music they performed was written! The other four masses which the book contained were such as one would expect Palestrina to have written while at St Agapit's—one for Easter (*Ad coenam Agni*), another for the feast of Corpus Christi (*O Regem coeli*) and two for general use, *Virtute magna* and *Gabriel archangelus*.

These works are of particular interest as showing the technical mastery Palestrina had acquired while still a young man, and his intimate knowledge of the northern schools, for although they were not published until he was twenty-nine, it is certain that a good deal of their music may date back to even ten years earlier.

The magnificent plainsong theme of the *Ecce sacerdos magnus* is treated brilliantly, with every kind of contrapuntal resource, and the same may be said of the *Virtute magna;* there is some very ingenious canonic writing in *Ad coenam Agni*, and the influence of Josquin des Prés is noticeable in *O Regem coeli* (perhaps the earliest of these masses). But there is as much difference between their music and that of the works of Palestrina's mature period as between *Rienzi* and *Tristan*.

Pope Julius was delighted with this 'musical offering' and expressed his appreciation in very practical fashion. He made the composer a member of the Pontifical Choir. This at first sight might seem a curious reward for a man who was an organist, a composer and a choirmaster, but not a singer. (Tradition says that he had a poor, weak tenor voice.) But the choir was a highly privileged, exclusive body, membership of which was a much-coveted honour. In the ranks of its thirty-two members many well-known musicians—Spanish, French and Italian—were to be found from time to time. The pay was ten scudi a month with various other emoluments, in money and kind.

One of the many prerogatives of the choir was apparently to be allowed some say in the election of a new member, whenever a vacancy occurred. But they were not consulted at all in this matter, for the choir secretary put it on record that Palestrina was admitted 'by order of our lord the pope, without examination and without the assent of the singers.' And, to make matters worse, there had been no vacancy. It is evident that they could see no reason why he should have been elected, and the fact that the composer of the *Papae Marcelli* Mass was not 'examined' doubtless rankled in their minds. The pope, of course, had enrolled him with a view to obtaining some new compositions for the choir's use, and this also would have been a grievance, since several of the members were composers who considered themselves as quite capable of writing all that was needful.

The appointment was made in January 1555, Palestrina relinquishing, of course, his post with the Julian Choir, where he was succeeded by the Florentine musician Giovanni Animuccia. Three months later Pope Julius died and was succeeded by Marcellus II, during whose transitory reign of only three weeks an incident occurred which probably had a great influence on Palestrina as a creative musician. The new pope was a saintly man bent on many reforms, especially in the musical services of the church. Elected in Holy Week, and presiding at the solemn functions taking place during that time, he seems to have been perturbed, while at the Good Friday ceremonies in the Sistine Chapel, to observe the perfunctory and light way in which the music was performed. Returning to the Vatican he took the somewhat unusual step of summoning the Papal Choir to his presence and addressing them. The gist of his speech to the singers has been preserved in the archives, where the papal secretary notes:

The pope himself, having summoned the singers to his presence, enjoined on them that whatever was performed on those holy days when the mysteries of the Passion and Death of the Saviour were celebrated, must be sung in a suitable manner, with properly modulated voices, and so that everything could be both heard and understood properly [*audiri atque percipi possent*].

There can be little doubt that Palestrina was profoundly impressed with the pope's personality and his earnestness, as well as by the artistic soundness of his remarks, especially the phrase *audiri atque percipi*. The impression was deepened by Marcellus's death so soon afterwards, and it is quite probable that from this moment Palestrina resolved to write a mass which should both honour the pope's memory and conform to his liturgical ideal.

The death of Marcellus, however, was to have far-reaching consequences in another direction. His successor Paul IV (Cardinal Carafa) was also filled with zeal for reforms in all directions where abuses might have crept in. His activities extended to the Pontifical Choir, where to his dismay he found married men with families, infringing the rule that all members must be single men and whenever possible in minor clerical orders, thus being eligible to take some part in the liturgical ritual—such as reading the epistles, gospels, etc.—as well as singing. Another cause of offence was that some of the choir members had taken to secular composition, writing the new, fashionable madrigals which had superseded the older pieces such as the *frottole*. And they had advertised themselves as church musicians in the publication of such music.

Palestrina himself, in 1555, had apparently issued a book of madrigals, on the title-page of which he was described in large type as being a member of the Papal Choir.[1] So he and two others (Ferrabosco and Barri) had to go. They were, however, given pensions of six scudi a month, this in Palestrina's case being exceptionally generous, since he had only been in the choir for about six months. This pension was eventually increased to the full pay (ten scudi) of an active member, in return for providing some music for the choir's use. This matter of the pension also caused resentment in the choir; indeed it was said that the latter had a hand in Palestrina's dismissal.

Just afterwards he had a serious illness which early bio-graphers attributed to disappointment and worry over this matter. But there is no ground for assuming this: he had his pension and, as previously pointed out, a certain private income, and therefore did not lack means of subsistence. Moreover, at the age of thirty, he had already made a reputation as a brilliant young musician, who would have no difficulty in finding a new post.

He had not long to wait. The musical affairs of the Lateran basilica (St John Lateran, the cathedral church of Rome) had been in an unsatisfactory state since Orlande de Lassus had relinquished his appointment as musical director there in the previous year (1554). The post was in abeyance for the moment, and the music was superintended by the archpriest of the basilica, Cardinal Farnese. Whether Palestrina actually applied for the appointment or whether he was invited to take up the work by the cardinal is not certain, but before he entered upon his duties he had to make sure that his papal pension would not be allowed to lapse, upon which point the chapter of St Peter's reassured him.

[1] No trace of this edition has survived, although its original existence seems fairly certain.

Exactly when he assumed his new duties is also uncertain, but an entry in the archives of the Lateran basilica records a payment for the making of a *cotta* (surplice) for 'ms. Io. mᵒ di cappella' in October 1555, and it is more than probable that the 'ms. Io' refers to Palestrina.

Although he remained there until 1560, his third son, Iginio, being born during this period, in 1557 or 1558, the appointment proved neither a lucrative nor a happy one. The pay was small: six scudi a month, and there was nothing to be made out of boarding and lodging the boys (a usual perquisite of the choir-master), since they were in the charge of a tenor named Bernardino, who may have been the composer's brother already referred to and who had perhaps transferred his services from St Peter's to St John's.[1]

The times were troubled: Rome suffered greatly through the war with Spain, and a financial stringency began to make itself felt even in high places. Consequently the choir was limited in numbers, and in other ways the music of the basilica was affected. Nevertheless Palestrina reorganized it as far as possible, bringing in his son Rodolfo as a choirboy, thereby obtaining for the lad free board, lodging and education, and then set to work again at composition. During the first part of his service at St John's he doubtless completed the *Missa Papae Marcelli*, the *Missa brevis* and other masses, and revised many earlier compositions. From this period date also a setting of the *Lamentations*,[2] some Magnificats, possibly the *Improperia* and the hymn *Crux fidelis*. A treasured possession of the Lateran is the famous MS., Codex 59, in which is

[1] Or he may have been the fellow-choirboy with Palestrina at Santa Maria Maggiore, whose name, with that of Palestrina and four others, is recorded in the archives of that basilica.

[2] The lessons (taken from the Prophet Jeremiah) belonging to the nocturnal offices of Holy Week.

to be found, in Palestrina's own hand, the manuscript of part of these *Lamentations* and other works. During those years, too, a number of madrigals from his pen found their way into the collections by different composers published in various cities.

Reference has already been made to the termination, by Palestrina himself, of his appointment at St John Lateran. He had never been satisfied with the provision for the carrying on of the music of the basilica, although, in justice to the chapter, it must be said that the bad times—partly due to the war being waged against the Spaniards in Italy—necessitated the cutting down of expenses. But, like many a church musician since, he may have been under the impression that the musical services had to bear the brunt of any financial retrenchment. And his own emoluments he probably considered insufficient, for it is at this time that we find him selling wine—he was, in fact, supplying it to the chapter (apparently for sacramental purposes) at so much the barrel. Matters came to a head with the decision of the canons to make certain alterations in the training and providing for the choirboys. What happened is told in quaint fashion by a resolution which appears in the minute-book of the capitular meetings under date of 3rd August 1560:

The canons deputed to administer the affairs of the choir having reported that Master Joannes Petraloysius, director of the said choir, had gone off at a moment's notice [*pene improviso*] taking his son with him, because he would not abide by the recent decree of his superior authority that nothing beyond 25 julii per month be allowed for the boys' victuals, it was unanimously resolved that the canons aforesaid should find and elect another in place of the said Master Joannes.

It was not until the following March that Palestrina found himself again in the service of the church. There are no details of any kind available as to what occupied his energies during those eight months; doubtless he looked after his little properties and was busy, as usual, with composition, perhaps preparing some of the motets which were to be published two years later, in a volume dedicated to Cardinal Carpi. The latter, a friend and counsellor of all the popes in whose reigns he lived, was another of those princes of the church who recognized Palestrina's genius: his interest in the composer had even taken the form of becoming godfather to his eldest son, named Rodolfo after him.[1]

On 1st March 1561 the chapter of Santa Maria Maggiore elected Palestrina as master of that choir where, twenty-four years earlier, he had been a chorister. Here too, as at St John Lateran, there seems to have been a regime of financial stringency, and for much the same reasons: the choir at one time had to be reduced to only four (adult) singers, and the choirmaster's pay to two-thirds the customary amount. But with Palestrina's advent an effort seems to have been made to revive the old musical establishment: the 'cut' in pay was restored, and also customary emoluments in connection with the care and training of boys, the choir being augmented to nearly its original strength. We can well believe that the chapter welcomed the return to the basilica of the gifted musician who had received his musical training there as a boy.

Soon after he had settled down to this new appointment a fresh worry awaited Palestrina. His pension from the Papal Choir was in danger. The choir funds were low, and a new member had to be provided for. It was therefore proposed to suspend the pensions of Palestrina and Ferrabosco, the only two who now received such payments. However, the composer's commercial instinct seems to have come to his rescue

[1] Some quotations from the dedicatory address to the cardinal which appeared in this publication have been given in a previous chapter.

with an idea. He promptly made a present to the choir of some new music—new, that is, in the sense that it had not been heard before, although probably written years earlier. As these offerings included some motets and the brilliant Hexachord Mass (afterwards published in 1570), it was doubt-less thought at the papal court that Palestrina was worth retaining, and therefore the pension was continued, and even augmented later on.

He seems to have remained at Santa Maria Maggiore until the spring of the year 1567—perhaps a little longer (the exact date at which he relinquished the post is not certain). But in 1564 an event happened which may have led to his resigna-tion. In that year Palestrina found a new patron, Cardinal Ippolito d' Este. The latter, immensely wealthy and a great lover of the arts, had built the famous villa at Tivoli which bears his name, and there he maintained a private musical establishment. During the summer of 1564, from July to September, Palestrina, at the cardinal's invitation, directed musical performances at the villa, apparently obtaining leave of absence from Santa Maria Maggiore by providing a deputy, an arrangement doubtless facilitated by his princely patron. About this time the composer seems to have become somewhat dissatisfied with church work, partly owing to the difficult conditions which were arising in such employment, and still more because of the poor financial reward. Moreover, the papal policy seemed to be in favour, since the Tridentine Council had closed its deliberations, of further simplification in liturgical music, with the implication that the duties (and salaries) of choirmasters, even in the leading churches, were likely to be of less account. Added to all this, life in Rome and the surrounding country was far from pleasant in many ways, owing to the continual wars waged in the kingdom.

It is not surprising, therefore, if Palestrina's thoughts perhaps turned towards the idea of becoming musical director at one of those magnificent courts maintained by secular nobles or princes in other parts of Italy, or in foreign countries: in such an appointment he would still be able to compose for the church, since to these establishments some great basilica or cathedral, or else a private chapel, was always attached.

Opportunities in this direction were to present themselves later; in the meantime a new offer of work in Rome came to hand. One of the results of the deliberations of the Council of Trent in 1563 was the decision to found a Roman seminary, where students could be educated for the priesthood, and to which sons of the laity might also be admitted. At this new institution, inaugurated in 1565, a feature of the curriculum was to be a thorough course in musical theory and liturgical music, especially plainsong. Palestrina was offered the post of music master in the new establishment, and seeing an opportunity of giving up church work, and also continuing at the Villa d' Este, accepted the offer, taking up his duties either at the end of 1565 or early in the following year.

Nevertheless he did not immediately sever his connection with Santa Maria Maggiore, probably remaining as titular director until the end of 1566 or early in 1567. He was certainly no longer there in April 1567, because, curiously enough, the archives of St John Lateran for that date reveal the fact that he returned there to assist in the Holy Week music of this church, the chapter of which had evidently agreed to let bygones be bygones. As an illustration of how payment in kind, instead of money, was still customary in those days, it may be mentioned that Palestrina, according to the chapter book, received for his help a pair of goats!

The pay as music master to the seminary was small, but his two elder sons, Rodolfo and Angelo, were admitted to it as scholars, receiving free board and lodging, full education and apparently even clothing. At this time the eldest, Rodolfo, was about sixteen years old, and his younger brother Angelo fourteen.

The musical establishment at the Villa d' Este comprised a small orchestra—of viols, lutes, trumpets and trombones—two organs and a choir, the performers being the finest available to the wealthy cardinal. During his stay each year Palestrina, like Liszt three centuries later, doubtless found inspiration in the marvellous situation of the villa and its garden, which has been described as one of the three or four most beautiful in the world.

Some of the last secular madrigals written by him may date from this period, composed for the entertainment of the cardinal and his guests, while his masses and motets would be sung during the services held in the chapel of the villa. And several of the motets which appeared in the collection dedicated to the cardinal (published in 1569) may date from those summer days at Tivoli).

In the following year (1568) an opportunity of leaving Rome presented itself. The Emperor Maximilian II, through his ambassador in Rome, offered Palestrina the post of musical director at his court in Vienna. The composer was asked to name his own terms and promptly asked a yearly salary equal to about twice as much as his combined earnings—the papal pension and the appointments at the seminary and the Villa d' Este. In all probability it was not altogether Palestrina's commercial instincts which made him demand this big sum: in spite of his dissatisfaction with affairs in Rome, he always regarded it as his spiritual and artistic home, which he would leave only if the inducement was so tempting that he could not well refuse it. Efforts were made to persuade him to reconsider his terms, but without success, and the negotiations were dropped. Probably Palestrina was not altogether sorry.

During this year a new interest was brought into his life, one destined to bring him both artistic pleasure and profit. This was the beginning of an association with Duke Guglielmo Gonzaga of Mantua, an amateur musician who had been trained as executant and composer under the best masters and maintained a first-rate private musical establishment. The two seem to have met only on one occasion when the duke, years later, visited Rome; but they maintained, as we have already seen, a friendly correspondence from time to time. Such of Palestrina's letters as have been preserved show a perfect blend of the courtier, the musician and the business man.

Their acquaintance, which extended over twenty years and terminated only with the duke's death, began when, through the offices of a mutual friend,[1] Palestrina, as we have already seen, was invited by the duke to compose a mass for the opening of the new church of Santa Barbara in Mantua. Doubtless he was rather perturbed at hearing nothing for several months after dispatching the music, when a messenger arrived in Rome with a letter from the duke, assuring him that the music had pleased; and more satisfactory still, there was a gift of fifty ducats accompanying the letter. This same year (1568) the duke's brother Scipio Gonzaga, Patriarch of Jerusalem, while staying at the Villa d' Este, saw there two of Palestrina's motets: these so delighted him that they were at once sent to the duke, the result being a further commission to Palestrina—to compose motets to words selected by the duke himself.

Just at this time he had a somewhat serious illness, of which he informs the duke when sending the motets (in December 1568).

[1] Don Annibale Cappello, a cleric residing in Rome.

CHAPTER V

MASTER OF THE MUSIC AT THE VATICAN BASILICA

EIGHTEEN months later we find Palestrina moving into a new house,[1] having (in May 1570) bought it from the relations of his friend Canon Attilio Ceci of St John Lateran. The price of the property was 725 scudi, with an annual tax or ground rent of 4 scudi, 12 bajocchi. Hardly had he settled down there when another event necessitated a change to a fresh dwelling.

Animuccia, the director of the Julian Choir at St Peter's, had died, and Palestrina, who perhaps during the last four or five years regretted the cessation of any regular church work on his own part, was offered the post. His reputation at this time was such, indeed, that any vacant position of this kind was his if he cared to take it, and the satisfaction of the authorities at having secured his services was shown by the fact that the salary was at once raised from eight to ten scudi per month, with thirty scudi a year towards a lodging and three scudi a month for boarding and lodging the choirboys. The acceptance of the latter obligation meant taking a larger house. A suitable one was found quite close to St Peter's at the corner of a little street (subsequently named Calle del Palestrina and now demolished) which led to the Piazza della Sagrestia di San Pietro. In this, which Palestrina seems to have rented at

[1] It is just possible that he may have moved into this earlier, as Casimiri has discovered entries in some church archives relating to rent paid by Palestrina from 1568, for a house which may have been the one referred to.

50

thirty-six scudi a year, he now took up his residence some time in 1571 with his wife, sons, three or four choirboys and a private pupil: here, in fact, he spent the remainder of his life, passing away in the house on the Feast of the Purification, 2nd February 1594.

The older biographers assert that Palestrina, from the time he succeeded Animuccia at St Peter's, also continued the musical work founded by the latter at the oratory of St Philip Neri. The saint, a firm believer in the power of music as an aid to devotion, had some years previously enlisted Animuccia (who like himself was a Florentine) among his helpers at the newly founded oratory. The musician had gathered others of his profession around him, had written special music—*laudi spirituali*,[1] motets and similar works—regularly conducting performances at which these and other religious music formed the programme, with the result that the oratory became renowned as a centre of musical activity.

All this was carried on by Animuccia and his colleagues without any pecuniary reward whatever. But there is no evidence at all to show that Palestrina continued it:[2] as we know, he was not one to work for nothing, even for a saint. However, before we accuse him of worldliness or avarice, we must remember that whereas Animuccia had no mission as a composer, Palestrina was quite conscious of his own destiny, which he knew required both time and money for its

[1] A species of sacred song in which popular melodies were adapted to words in praise of the Saviour's love and suffering, and in honour of the Blessed Virgin.

[2] Cametti points out that the archives of the oratory at this time make no mention whatever of Palestrina; neither does his name occur in the earliest biographies of St Philip Neri. This would hardly be the case had he become intimately associated with the work of the oratory.

fulfilment. Like Wagner, he probably took the view that the world ought at least to provide its geniuses with the means of living in decent comfort.

Nevertheless the saint and the musician, two of Rome's outstanding figures at this time, must have known and admired each other. St Philip, a great music-lover, could hardly fail to realize the commanding genius of Palestrina, and the latter, worldly in some respects, had a deeply religious nature and, like so many others in Rome, no doubt came under the influence of the spiritual force radiating from the founder of the Oratorians.

It is most likely that some of Palestrina's music would be sung during those great public reunions held at the oratory, and the composer may have occasionally directed performances there. Raugel, in his biography, says, on what authority he does not state, that the composer wrote a few *laudi* and two motets (for three voices) for the oratory: *Jesu, Rex admirabilis* and *Jesu, sommo conforto*.

In later years he was apparently associated with the confraternity of the Trinity, a sodality attached to the oratory, and (according to Raugel) he was paid eighty scudi for acting as musical director to the confraternity for a year, receiving on another occasion thirty-three scudi for directing their music during Lent.

At the end of this year, when Palestrina was back at St Peter's, the victory over the Turks at Lepanto, which set all Rome rejoicing, inspired him to compose the madrigal *Le selv' avea*; this was sung during the celebrations, probably in an open-air procession.

The next eight years (from 1572 to 1580) were destined to be a tragic period in the composer's life. Rome and the surrounding countryside were swept by pestilence and famine, due in part to the ravages of continual warfare. In a succes-

sion of epidemics, which seem to have corresponded to a
virulent influenza, Palestrina suffered in turn the loss of his
two elder sons, Rodolfo and Angelo, his brother Silla (and,
according to Raugel, his brother Bernardino also) and, heaviest
blow of all, his wife, while he himself endured sickness and
privation.

Palestrina was justly proud of his three sons, all of whom
inherited some part of his own musical gift. He had social
ambitions for them and was preparing to launch them out on
successful careers as soon as opportunity should serve. The
two elder boys seem to have been particularly brilliant: both had
benefited by the excellent Roman seminary education they had
received and were well versed in the classics, philosophy, logic,
etc. All three were taught music by their father. Rodolfo
was a fine executant; Angelo gave promise of becoming a
composer of repute; the youngest, Iginio (only fourteen years
of age at this time), ultimately became a doctor of law, but he
too was not without musical talent. Such pride did Palestrina
take in their musical abilities that in the book of his own motets
issued in 1572 were included one by Rodolfo, another by
Angelo, as well as two by his younger brother Silla, whom
he had also taught.

Rodolfo's work [1] was a setting (in five parts) of the offertory
Confitebor tibi Domine, Angelo's contribution a double motet
(also in five voices), *Circuire possum Domine*, Silla being represented by a five-part motet, *Domine Pater*, and a six-part
Nunc dimittis, the latter quite an admirable piece of writing.
It is quite likely, of course, that all four pieces were well
'edited' by Palestrina himself, for he appears to have had a
motive beyond exhibiting the family talent in publishing them.
This 1572 volume was dedicated to Duke Guglielmo, as it
contained two motets—*Gaude Barbara beata* and *Beata Barbara*

[1] A madrigal by Rodolfo, *Ahi, letizia fugace*, also exists.

ad locum—specially written for the Mantuan church. A copy
was immediately dispatched to the duke, with a suitable letter,
perhaps in the hope that it might draw attention to these
talented relatives and possibly lead to some profitable employ/
ment for them. If this were really the plan, it did not mis/
carry. The duke, who had heard from another source of
Rodolfo's talents, and that he was a personable young man (he
was just twenty/two at this time), decided to offer him the
post of organist at Santa Barbara, where a fine new instrument
was being installed at the duke's expense.[1] But two months
later Rodolfo died in the epidemic which carried off 200 in
the parish of St Peter's alone. Three months later, in January
1573, Silla Pierluigi, to whom the composer was much
attached, also died.

After the loss of Rodolfo, Palestrina's family hopes and
ambitions naturally centred in Angelo. Next door to the
house in which the family lived, before his return to St Peter's,
dwelt a certain Giovanni Uberti, by whose daughter Doralice
the youthful Angelo had evidently been attracted, for a
marriage was now arranged between the two. The match
was an excellent one both socially and financially. The
Uberti were apparently of good family, the bride's uncle being
a doctor of laws, and the young lady brought a handsome
dowry to young Pierluigi.

This was in 1573, the same year in which the famous
Improperia were heard during Holy Week at St Peter's. The
exact date of their composition is not certain, but the manu/
script, in Palestrina's own hand, preserved in the famous

[1] The intermediary in this matter seems to have been a certain
Bishop Odescalco, because in a letter to the duke informing him of
Rodolfo's death he speaks of the latter as 'of very good morals . . .
a most gifted musician and player on various instruments. . . . I
believe he would have been to your Excellency's liking.'

Codex 59 now at St John Lateran (the only specimen of his musical calligraphy in existence), had attached to it the names of singers known to have been members of the Julian Choir at this date, so that we may not be far wrong in assigning the music to 1572 or 1573 instead of the earlier date sometimes suggested. To the same period belongs another book of *Lamentations*. His growing fame as a composer at this time apparently made the authorities of Santa Maria Maggiore desirous of having him back there as musical director. They were willing to pay double the salary he was getting at St Peter's, an offer which must have caused a struggle between Palestrina's commercial and artistic instincts. The Vatican basilica was, of course, the more important of the two churches, ecclesiastically; moreover, he held a privileged position there and had an exceptionally fine choir. On the other hand, he could not hope for such a salary there, as the chapter of St Peter's, when he informed them of the offer, declined to pay such an amount to retain his services. Ultimately Palestrina was able to adjust the conflicting claims of money and art by accepting a fifty per cent increase of pay to remain at his post.

The next blow to fall upon him was the death (in December 1575) of Angelo, who left a daughter, a son being born posthumously. His death also involved Palestrina in financial worry. As was the patriarchal fashion of the times, he had charge of all the family's worldly possessions. According to the law Angelo's widow was entitled to the return of her dowry, and Palestrina, who always seems to have spent money freely, had apparently no resources out of which to effect this; the sum had therefore to be borrowed at interest.

The loss of his two eldest sons and his brother made the continuance of the Pierluigi family dependent on the surviving male member, his son Iginio. Palestrina was accordingly anxious to see the latter settled in life, and although

Iginio was only about eighteen or nineteen at this time, a marriage was arranged for him with a certain Virginia Guarnecci, the wedding taking place on the Feast of the Assumption (15th August) in 1576, at the church of San Lorenzo (in the Trajan Forum). This match was also satisfactory from the social and financial point of view, and with the young lady's dowry and the help of proceeds from the sale of a vineyard and a house, the money borrowed to pay out Angelo's widow was redeemed!

It may here be mentioned that Palestrina's desire for the continuance of the Pierluigi family was destined to be unfulfilled. Iginio, after the death of his wife, in 1608, aspired, like his father, to the priesthood, and actually entered that state. Retiring to the town of Palestrina, he was appointed canon of St Agapit's on 17th September 1610, but died three weeks later, on 9th October.

Of his eight children only two males survived, Tommaso, who followed his father into the priesthood and also became in turn a canon of the cathedral in his ancestral town, and Gregorio. The latter married, but of his family only one son grew to manhood, Agapito, and he, following his uncle and grandfather, also became a priest, dying in 1677 as a canon of the cathedral whose name he bore. With him the male line of the Pierluigis became extinct; but through one of Gregorio's daughters, who married, there are to this day descendants of the composer in Italy.

As an instance of the esteem and the social honour accorded to the composer, it may be mentioned that Cardinal Sirleto stood godfather to his grandson Tommaso at the latter's baptism.

The deaths of his sons and his brother seem to have affected Palestrina's creative work, for nothing was published by him from 1575 to 1581. He may have had neither means nor inclination to go on with his music, but there was perhaps a further reason. One of the findings of the Council of Trent was a recommendation for the thorough revision of the liturgy. The Breviary and the Missal were first dealt with, and then came the turn of the Gradual. A papal brief issued by Gregory XIII on 28th October 1577 decreed that the plainchant must be 'purged of many barbarisms, obscurities, contradictions, superfluities and wrong notes (*mali suoni*).' These had arisen firstly through the many errors made by copyists during the centuries that had elapsed since Gregory the Great had first collated the plainchant, and secondly in more recent times by printers. Moreover, many local variations existed in various parts of Italy and abroad. The matter was placed in the hands of Cardinal Sirleto, who naturally asked Palestrina to take up the work and appointed Zoilo as his assistant.

With the enthusiasm for this ancient music of the church which Palestrina's works show, he doubtless welcomed the task as a congenial one, until he realized its herculean nature. Both musicians struggled with the work for some years, then abandoned it. The question of this revision became, while they were engaged upon it, a controversial one. Philip II of Spain, always ready to interfere in church matters, opposed any alteration in the Gradual, going so far as to inform the pope that he would forbid the revised version entry into his kingdom.

It was not until nearly half a century later, indeed, that a new Gradual, known as the Medicean edition, made its appearance, and very little, if any, of Palestrina's and Zoilo's work appeared therein.

While busied with this ungrateful task Palestrina, in 1578, had a serious illness (in a letter to Duke Guglielmo he speaks of being 'many days in bed'), no doubt caused by one of those influenza-like visitations which, two years later, dealt him the worst blow of all. His wife, who had shared his joys and sorrows for nearly thirty-three years, and to whom he was undoubtedly devoted, was carried off in the worst epidemic Rome had known. It must have been of a terrible kind,[1] for it is said that 10,000 persons died in Rome during six months, Lucrezia Pierluigi being one of 500 victims in the parish of St Peter's alone during July and August, her death taking place on 28th July 1580.

Palestrina, although comforted by being surrounded by his son, daughter-in-law, their children and his other grand-children, Angelo's son and daughter, was stunned by his loss. In his anguish of mind he resolved to abandon music and enter the priesthood, presenting to Pope Gregory a petition in November of the same year, in which he says that, moved 'ex devotionis zelo et fervore,' he desired to proceed to clerical orders and then to the priesthood. The pope, much gratified by Palestrina's wish, promptly issued a brief directed to 'our beloved son, Joannes Petraloysius, a layman of Palestrina,' in which the required permission was immediately granted, adding that he might be ordained priest with the rank of Master of the Music at the basilica ('ad titulum magisterii Capelle Musices Basilice'). This was dated 13th November 1580, and on 7th December the composer received the tonsure, that is to say, he enjoyed clerical status as distinguished from the laity, the ceremony taking place at the church of St Sylvester on the Quirinal, Cardinal Sirleto's church. Pope Gregory, as a further mark of his pleasure at this step on Palestrina's part, bestowed upon him a vacant benefice attached to the cathedral of Santa Maria Maggiore at Ferrentina: it did not involve any residence there and carried with it a yearly stipend of twenty-

[1] Cametti says that the pestilence was known as *mal di castrone* (literally 'sheep disease').

four gold ducats. The papal bull conferring this, in which Palestrina is designated a *clericus*, bears the date 18th January 1581. He should now have been preparing to be admitted to minor orders, as the next stage towards the priesthood.[1] Whether he actually took any further steps towards this end is at least uncertain, because a few weeks later he met a well-to-do widow, Virginia Dormuli, to whom he must have proposed almost immediately, because notice was given of an intended marriage between the two on 24th February 1581. The ceremony took place on the 28th of the following month, eight months only having elapsed since the death of his first wife, and less than three since he had assumed clerical status. Palestrina was, of course, not infringing the law of the church in any way by doing this; the *clericale caracter* did not impose celibacy upon the recipient so long as he proceeded no further.

The wedding took place very quietly and privately at Signora Dormuli's own house, a somewhat curious proceeding in view of Palestrina's important position at St Peter's. Cametti suggests that the lady might have had some infirmity preventing her from leaving the house, but this seems unlikely. Her husband had died some five years before, at the early age of thirty-seven, leaving his widow a prosperous skin and furrier's business, which had the valuable monopoly of supplying the papal court. The stock in hand and other assets made Signora Dormuli's fortune worth about 1,500 scudi, with a house, apart from the goodwill of the establishment. She was probably not more than forty, possibly younger, at the time of the marriage to Palestrina, who was then about fifty-six.

[1] The successive steps to be taken were first the admission to the four minor orders: doorkeeper, reader, exorcist and acolyte; then the ordination to major orders: sub-deacon, deacon and finally the priesthood.

Casimiri is probably near the truth when he says that the composer had more than one reason for keeping the marriage as secret as possible. But Pope Gregory must soon have known of it, and we may wonder if he allowed Palestrina to retain the cathedral benefice.

In all probability the chief attraction for Palestrina in this second marriage was the prospect of living in comfort for the rest of his life and of commanding sufficient funds to carry out his one great aim—the publication of such music as still remained in manuscript, and the opportunity to compose and publish still more. If we look at dates, it will be seen that from this time volumes of his compositions appeared in quick succession, one, sometimes two, each year, whereas previously the gaps between publication of the earlier books were often of several years' duration.

For Signora Dormuli the marriage represented a certain social advancement, from being merely the widow of a respect-able *bourgeois* trader in fur to the position of wife of a celebrated composer, who occupied a social status in Rome probably unusual for a musician, counting as he did princes of the church and the laity as well as many high ecclesiastical dignitaries among his personal friends. It is not known how the marriage turned out from the domestic point of view, for beyond the fact of its existence we can dis-cover no further mention of the matter. Apparently no children were born of the union, and all we know is that Signora Dormuli-Pierluigi survived her husband by nearly seventeen years, dying in December 1610, two months after Iginio.

But the marriage had an immediate and surprising conse-quence. Palestrina 'went into business.' He saw a chance of making money out of his wife's furriery, and he seems to have done so. The facts brought to light in connection with this commercial venture on the composer's part are somewhat remarkable.[1]

In addition to furs, skins, and perhaps leather, were sold at the establishment, which was evidently, for the times, one of considerable size, since the stock, at the time of Signora Dormuli's marriage to Palestrina, was valued at 900 scudi. The first thing Palestrina did was to enter into partnership with a young man, Annibale Gagliardi, who was employed in the business, apparently as a worker dealing with the materials. The composer furnished a capital of 1,000 scudi, Gagliardi continuing his practical services and receiving in return one-third of the profits. Palestrina, one may suppose, was the general manager and attended to the finances. The deed of partnership was for five years, and on expiry it was renewed for a similar period, with a doubled capital, Signora Pierluigi and Gagliardi now investing 500 scudi each in the business. Three years later the former withdrew her share, and lent it to her husband, under a legal agreement wherein he undertook to pay eight per cent interest for the money! Apparently he borrowed this sum in order to complete the payment for the house near St Peter's into which he had moved on returning to the Vatican basilica. The two partners made the business prosper: the partnership deed stipulated that 200 scudi must be put to reserve yearly, and 1,300 scudi of the money so accumulated was in 1589 invested by the purchase of land (in the Borgo Sant' Angelo close to the city walls), upon which two houses were built by the partners and let out at a good profit.

Palestrina's life must have been one of considerable activity in these years. In addition to the business he had, of course,

[1] The matter is discussed at length in Cametti's *Palestrina e il suo commercio delle pelliccerie* (Rome, Società Romana di Storia patria, 1921).

his duties at St Peter's necessitating daily attendance there (although he might occasionally employ the services of a deputy), while over and above these matters he resumed his creative work with even greater ardour than before. This period saw the production of some of his very greatest master, pieces—masses such as the *Assumpta est Maria, Aeterna Christi munera, Ecce ego Joannes* and *Te Deum laudamus,* such motets as *Surge illuminare, Super flumina, Sicut cervus,* great hymns like the *Vexilla Regis,* the sequence *Lauda Sion* and the magnificent *Stabat Mater.*

These last thirteen years of his life, from 1581 to 1594, saw the publication, no doubt with the money obtained from the business, of no less than sixteen collections of various works —three volumes of masses, three of motets, three of madrigals, two of offertories, two of litanies, one of lamentations, one of hymns and one of magnificats—containing between them nearly 400 compositions. And still there remained a good number unpublished at his death.

Even after his second marriage Palestrina suffered further bereavements. Before the end of 1581 three of his grand, children, the two orphans left by Angelo (whose widow had married again) and an infant son of Iginio were all dead.

Once again, in 1583, he entertained the idea of leaving Rome and settling elsewhere. His patron, Duke Guglielmo Gonzaga, who had for some years past employed as his musical director Francesco Soriano (a pupil of Palestrina), desired to make a change, Soriano having shown himself rather dilatory in the discharge of his duties. The Mantuan ambassador at Rome, acting on instructions, consulted Palestrina as to the choice of a successor. The latter suggested Zoilo or Marenzio, and both having declined the post, the ambassador was sur, prised to receive a hint from Palestrina that he himself might consider settling at Mantua. Naturally the duke would have been more than pleased to welcome such an illustrious musician to the court, and negotiations were at once begun for the acquisition of his services. In the course of these we learn that Palestrina's salary at St Peter's had been augmented since 1578 to fifteen scudi a month (nearly double that paid to Animuccia), while his pension from the Papal Choir had also been increased in consideration of the music furnished by him from time to time.

The terms he finally demanded were 200 ducats per annum, free board and lodging for his household of seven persons— himself, his wife, his son and daughter-in-law, their child and two servants—and all the expenses of the journey from Rome to Mantua. The duke declined the offer on the ground of being unable to afford this expense, so once again Palestrina remained in Rome.

However, apprehensive lest their friendly relations might have been disturbed by this matter, he made haste to send the duke a copy of his latest masterpiece, the *Song of Solomon* settings, as soon as these were published a few months later, in 1584. Perhaps the message of acknowledgment (sent through the duke's customary intermediary in Rome, Don Annibale Cappello) was none too cordial, so a further gift of music was presently dispatched—the motets in five parts (also pub- lished in this same year)—accompanied by a really amazing letter from Palestrina to his patron in which he writes: 'I do not like to think that my work should reach other hands before I had the benefit of that most prudent judgment of yours, such as none other possesses in this particular art of music; and had I been in your neighbourhood I should have liked to submit it to you for any suggestions as to improvement, before sending it to be printed.'[1]

[1] Cametti's wrath at this makes amusing reading: '. . . that he, the great master, famous in Italy and abroad, the creator of so many

It is not difficult to discern the motive underlying such a gross piece of flattery, which in all probability the duke, who seems to have been a man of intelligence, rated at its true worth. Some years had elapsed since Palestrina had received any commissions from the duke, and the letter was perhaps a subtle attempt to obtain some more. But nothing came of the idea, and a year later we find Palestrina writing again, lamenting that he was growing old (although only sixty at this time) and losing his skill at composition—perhaps another endeavour to induce sympathy and interest in a practical form. A last letter from him reached the duke just a month or so before the latter's death, in 1587. In it he informs the duke that he is sending him a singer for the latter's choir: this was a bass, formerly one of the papal singers.

---

masterpieces, should pretend to a mediocre amateur that if he had been nearer, etc. . . . . it is hard to believe that even at that time such flattery should deceive.'

CHAPTER VI

THE CLOSING YEARS

THE year 1584, as we have seen, was marked by the appearance of one of Palestrina's finest works, apart from the masses, the setting of the *Song of Solomon*. He had already, in 1581, or perhaps a little later, issued a work in somewhat similar vein, the series of *Canzoni spirituali* (twenty-six of them), in which are to be found settings of Petrarch's mystical stanzas to the Blessed Virgin ('Vergine bella che di sol vestita'), these forming the first eight of the collection.

Both these and the *Song of Solomon* found much public favour even during the composer's lifetime. The *Vergine*, as the 1581 work became known, was reprinted more than once, while the *Song of Solomon* went to nine editions in twenty years, the last (in 1613) being printed with a figured bass for organ, an eloquent commentary on the changed view of the musical world only twenty years after the composer's death.

Between these two works appeared others, a book of motets and one of masses. But it is not to be assumed that their contents represent music all actually composed at this time. Thus in the preface to this fourth book of masses Palestrina mentions that they have been selected from a number 'already written.' The book of motets was dedicated to a youthful nephew of the King of Poland, who had come to Rome at this time, to be created cardinal. No doubt the dedication was offered with an eye to business, in the hope of creating interest in his music in a new direction.

The dedication[1] of the masses just referred to was offered to Pope Gregory XIII, to whom he reiterates the essentially religious nature of his creative talent, affirming that intellectual gifts which are bestowed by God should always be used in His honour. 'And so I have wished above all,' he continues, 'to consecrate everything to the celebration of the divine praises, and nothing could be more acceptable to God than the prayers which accompany the most holy sacrifice of the Mass.'

His creative activities at this time in completing unfinished works, revising earlier ones and composing fresh music were indeed remarkable.

In addition to the publication already mentioned, another book of motets (for five voices) appeared in 1584, while during the following year four more masses saw the light, although only in the form of manuscript copies for the Papal Choir, these including the magnificent work founded upon the Ambrosian plainchant *Te Deum*, and one written upon themes from the composer's own great eight-part motet, *Dum complerentur*. And during the next three or four years there appeared, in the same choir-books, such masterpieces as the masses entitled *Assumpta est Maria, Ecce ego Joannes,* the five-part *Salve Regina* and *O sacrum convivium*, as well as more motets.

In the year 1585 there occurred a curious affair in which the Papal Choir was concerned and Palestrina's name involved. Briefly the facts seem to have been as follows: In May Antonio Boccapaduli,[2] the clerico-musician who held the post of director of the choir which Palestrina apparently coveted, called the members together, informing them that Palestrina was in-

[1] Cametti—rather uncharitably—remarks that this preface was apparently intended 'to show profound religious sentiment and to exhibit, under the veil of an ostentatious modesty, the composer's worth and diligence.'

[2] Cametti describes him as 'the irascible Boccapaduli.'

IVLIVS TERTIVS PONTIFEX MAX

PALESTRINA PRESENTING HIS MASSES TO POPE JULIUS III

The picture is taken from the frontispiece to the first volume of masses issued in 1554, and gives the earliest known portrait of the composer

triguing to obtain the directorship and had been canvassing for support among the choir personnel; he also accused one Tommaso Benigni, a junior singer, of being a ringleader in the matter by trying to influence others in favour of Palestrina.

The majority of the singers expressed indignation at all this: apparently there was always some sort of animosity against Palestrina in the choir ranks, probably because of his some-what unusual distinction in being styled 'composer to the choir,' and still more because, vague though this position was, he drew as much salary as they themselves, while doing considerably less. So the choir, which evidently had minor disciplinary powers over the members, fined Benigni nine scudi (a month's salary). A fortnight later Boccapaduli sum-moned the choir again and declared that Benigni had been unjustly accused, asking that the fine should be remitted. That same day the choir secretary reported the names of four senior members of the choir to the vicar-general, Cardinal Bonelli. Nothing more was heard for five months, when it was learned that these four members were to be suspended. Two were ultimately reinstated, the other two being dismissed.

In the story as recounted by earlier biographers Pope Sixtus V (who had been elected the previous April) was said to have been behind all this, in an endeavour to find out if the choir was willing to have Palestrina as director. But there is no evidence for the accusation, and certainly there was no need for any pope to be obliged to act in so curious a manner or to defer to the choir if he wished to make an appointment. Indeed, Sixtus V, some months later (in 1586), took the matter of the choir in hand and made very different dispositions from what might have been expected had he wished to appoint Palestrina.

The choir was under the joint control of a clerical prefect, in charge of disciplinary and other non-musical affairs, and a

technical musical director. Pope Sixtus now abolished the
former post and decreed that the latter should in future be held
in rotation, for one year, by the senior members of the choir.
This arrangement, of course, put an end to any further hopes
on Palestrina's part of obtaining the post which, it may be
pointed out, now became much less important.

In fairness to Palestrina it must be said that there is no
evidence to connect him directly with this mysterious affair.
Whatever his faults, he seems always to have been a man who
acted in a straightforward and honourable manner. In all
probability it was an intrigue by some well‚meaning but
injudicious friend, or friends, who, knowing how much the
composer would have liked the post, endeavoured to obtain
from the choir some expression of a desire to see him at their
head; armed with this it might then have been possible to
approach the pope.

As successive pontiffs did not see fit to set aside the rules in
favour of a musician whose pre‚eminence they all undoubtedly
recognized, there must have been some good reasons for their
attitude. In a sense the directorship of the Papal Choir may
have been the greatest distinction that a church musician
could win, for the choir was attached to the pope's private
chapel (the Sistine), where the congregation was the most
distinguished in Rome, being in fact the papal court, ecclesi‚
astical and lay. On the other hand, Palestrina enjoyed a
unique distinction in being considered composer to this choir,
an honour that had never previously been conferred on any
one else; also he was director of the choir belonging to the
principal basilica in Rome,[1] and therefore responsible for the

[1] He was no longer known as 'Master of the Julian Choir' but
as 'Master of the Music at the Vatican Basilica,' and a papal brief
of 1578 had confirmed him in that office for life, at the augmented
salary granted in 1575.

music performed at the most important public religious ceremonies in the Eternal City. Moreover, the combined salaries
from these two sources made an amount at least equal to what
he would have enjoyed as Papal Choir director.

Sixtus V was, no doubt, as appreciative of Palestrina's
musical genius as any of his predecessors, who in consequence
extended to him a toleration, in respect of such matters as his
treatment of the chapter of St John Lateran and his abandon-
ment of the idea of the priesthood, which might not have been
forthcoming to a musician of inferior quality.

To Pope Sixtus the composer dedicated the volume of the
splendid hymns [1] published in 1589, perhaps because one of
them was associated with a memorable occasion, in this year
(1585) of the choir affair, when the pontiff presided at the
solemn ceremony in the piazza of St Peter's during which the
great obelisk originally brought from Egypt by Caligula was
erected there. As the monolith, to the summit of which a
reliquary containing a fragment of the True Cross had been
affixed, slowly rose, the choir sang Palestrina's setting of the
Vexilla Regis, and when at last it was in position the great
crowd present fell on its knees, gazing upward at the relic,
while the singers chanted the beautiful verse 'O Crux ave,
spes unica.'

This ceremony affords a proof of the privileged position
Palestrina evidently enjoyed through the favour of the popes,
for although not the master of the Papal Choir, on this occasion
he seems to have been at its head: a contemporary account,
in a description of the scene, relates that in the grand procession
Palestrina led the pontifical singers, marching in front of them
as they sang his hymn.

About the same period Rome saw the beginnings of a social

[1] These hymns form a definite part of the liturgy of services such
as Vespers, Compline, Lauds, etc.

and intellectual movement among the musicians of the day, one result of which was the ultimate establishment of an institution from which the present Roman conservatoire of music, the Accademia Reale di S. Cecilia, is descended. It began with the formation (in 1584) of a body calling itself the Vertuosa Compagnia dei musici, whose members undertook to give mutual assistance, and apparently there was a certain religious side to its work, probably the obligation to see that members had proper burial with a sung requiem. Both church and secular musicians were admitted to the ranks of the association, which enjoyed the patronage of Pope Gregory XIII. Another activity was to undertake the publication of music written by its members, among whom was Palestrina, for his name appears in a volume of madrigals issued in 1589 entitled *Le gioje*.

Apparently there was some opposition to this Vertuosa Compagnia, especially from the Papal Choir, probably as a demonstration against Palestrina.

In the following year, under the pontificate of Sixtus V, we find mention of a Confraternità dei musici di Roma (which may have been a new body, as Sixtus V does not seem to have continued the papal patronage to the earlier society, or a reconstruction of the latter). According to Raugel a certain Canon Marino had founded a 'Congregazione di S. Cecilia' at the end of 1584, and it may be that the Confraternità was an amalgamation of the two: Cametti states that the conservatoire was evolved from the latter.

In 1588 an interesting event, one of which Palestrina may have been unaware, took place. This was the first publication in England of some of his music. Five of his madrigals were printed in a book entitled *Musica Transalpina*, a collection of madrigals mainly by Italian composers. In it was included a motet by Byrd, and so we find side by side the names of the

ROME IN PALESTRINA'S DAY

The illustration is taken from an old map of 1570 showing St. Peter's in course of reconstruction. The house where Palestrina lived for nearly a quarter of a century and died was probably situated in the street at the top left-hand corner of the picture

Italian master and the English musician who has sometimes been termed (quite wrongly, of course) the 'English Palestrina.' The collection was published by a certain Nicholas Yonge and printed by Thomas East, to whom Byrd had assigned the printing monopoly granted to himself and Tallis by Queen Elizabeth, and is described as:

Madrigales translated of foure, five, and sixe parts, chosen out of divers excellent Authors, with the first and second part of *La Verginella* made by Maister Byrd upon two Stanzas of Ariosto and brought to speake English with the rest.

Published by N. Yonge, in favour of such as take pleasure in Musick of voices.

Imprinted at London by Thomas East, the assigne of William Byrd 1588.

Cum Privilegio Regiae Maiestatis.

Nicholas Yonge (or Young) was a merchant in the City of London engaged in importing foreign goods (Burney calls him 'an Italian merchant'). He was also an enthusiastic patron of music and seems to have obtained a reputation as a connoisseur among his fellow-merchants and customers; in a lengthy dedicatory preface to Lord Talbot he says that he had been 'furnishing a great number of Gentlemen and Merchants of good accompt (as well of this realme as of forreine nations) with books of that kind [i.e. madrigals] yeerly sent me out of Italy and other places, which beeing for the most part Italian Songs, are for sweetness of Aire, verie well liked of all.' He also mentions that he was known for musical performances at his house,[1] and finally explains that the Italian and other words were 'translated by a Gentleman for his private delight.' In the collection Palestrina's name figures in two different ways—as Gio. Petraloysis Prenestino

[1] Probably the first performance in England of any work by Palestrina took place thus, at one of these private concerts.

and Gianetto Palestina. Yonge probably imagined these two names represented different composers.

These five of his madrigals were printed (the English titles being given in brackets): *Gioja m' abond' al cor* (*Joy so delights my heart*), *Amor, ben puoi* (*False Love now shoot*), *Perchè s'annida Amore* (*What meaneth Love to nest him*), *Amor, quando fioria* (*Sweet Love when hope*) and *Vestiva i colli* (quaintly entered thus: *Sound out my voyce* to the note of *Vestiv' i colli*).

Besides Palestrina and Byrd, sixteen other composers figure in this collection of forty madrigals—the latter word being used for the first time in England in this *Musica Transalpina*. They include Orlande de Lassus, Alfonso Ferrabosco and Luca Marenzio.

With the possible exception of one or two more madrigals published in this way, nothing by Palestrina seems to have been printed in this country until about 200 years later, when Dr Burney 'discovered' Palestrina and lauded him to English musicians (in the third volume of his *History of Music*, where he prints the motet *Exaltabo te Domine*).[1] Burney also brought from Rome and published here the *Stabat Mater* and other portions of the composer's music sung during Holy Week in the Sistine Chapel. Half a century later Vincent Novello, about the time of the Catholic Emancipation Act, began to publish some of the music of the masses and other liturgical works.

[1] Against the music he has the following note: 'In the copy whence this Motet was taken it is written in D minor, but it is so much more pleasing in F major that it seems to have been written in that key' (!).

CHAPTER VII

THE END

ONCE again anxiety concerning his pension from the Papal Choir may have beset Palestrina, from 1590 onwards, when no less than four popes in succession occupied the chair of St Peter during a period of less than two years following the death of Sixtus V in August 1590: Urban VII, whose reign of thirteen days holds the record for brevity; Gregory XIV (who was pope for ten and a half months); Innocent IV, who occupied the papal throne for two months, and finally Clement VIII. Fearful that all these changes might bring a pontiff unfavourable to his position as composer to the choir, Palestrina was assiduous in presenting new works for the use of the choir —no fewer than twenty motets, and amongst other things the eight-part *Stabat Mater*. It may well have been the last-named work which induced Clement VIII, in 1592, to show his appreciation of Palestrina's genius, by increasing his pension (or stipend) from the Papal Choir to sixteen scudi a month.

In the closing years of his life Palestrina was the recipient of an artistic tribute that must have been without precedent in those days (and indeed has seldom been repeated anywhere), affording a remarkable proof of the recognition accorded to his genius by his contemporaries. A number of musicians in Venetia, Lombardy and Tuscany joined together in this act of homage to one they deemed the master of them all, the leading spirit being the Veronese Giovanni Asola. He, with thirteen others, produced a musical offering, dedicated in terms of glowing eulogy to Palestrina, which took the form of a collection

73

of psalm settings, composed by themselves for Vespers (*Sacra omnia Solemnitate Psalmodia Vespertina, cum cantico B. Virginis a diversis in Arte Musica praestantissimis viris notatis musicis exornata*). It bore the dedication: 'Ad celeberrimum ac prae-stantissimum in arte musica coryphaeum D. Jo. Petrum Aloysium Praenestinum.'

Accompanying the music was a letter (dated 15th September 1592) signed by Asola, in which with much eloquence Palestrina was compared to 'an ocean of knowledge' and other composers to 'rivers whose life is bound up with the sea, into which they shed their tribute.' Palestrina replied with a witticism of which one would hardly suspect him. He sent back a little setting of a Vespers Antiphon[1] the words of which read: 'Vos amici mei estis si feceritis quae praecipio vobis, dixit Dominus' ('Ye are my friends, if ye do what I teach, saith the Lord').

In the following year, 1593, the composer seems to have contemplated retirement, probably in order to complete the publication of his many works which still remained in manu-script. For some of the latter he seems to have found a friend and patron, who either bore the cost of publication or con-tributed something towards it. This was a French Benedic-tine monk of noble family, Abbé de la Baume Saint-Amour, to whom the two books of offertories for the whole year, appear-ing in 1593, are dedicated. From the glowing expressions of gratitude to be found in the dedicatory preface one may reasonably infer that the abbé had expressed his admiration for the music in a welcome and practical form, otherwise the dedication would doubtless have been offered to some person of more exalted rank.

About this time Palestrina was in indifferent health, and

[1] To be found in the Commemoration of Apostles and Evangelists.

74

whether he had actually resigned his post at St Peter's or remained 'titular' while someone else did the work is not certain;
but towards the end of the year he had made up his mind to
leave Rome and end his days in his native town. At this
moment the post he had held at St Agapit's in his youth
happened to be vacant, his pupil and kinsman Cesare Veccia
having just died. Palestrina promised the cathedral chapter to
come and take temporary charge until a successor should be
appointed. But at the beginning of the new year, while preparing to leave Rome, and in the midst of superintending the
printing of his seventh book of masses, he was taken ill [1]
and died in a few days, on 2nd February 1594 (the Feast of
the Purification).

His funeral again furnished a proof of the esteem and respect
in which his genius was held. He was buried in old St
Peter's, at the foot of the altar of what was known as the
'Cappella nuova,' the leaden coffin being inscribed with the
famous phrase 'Musicae Princeps.' The obsequies were
attended, according to contemporary accounts,[2] by an immense
concourse of people. A few days later the Papal Choir sang
a solemn requiem for the repose of his soul.

Unfortunately no steps seem to have been taken to mark the
exact site of his grave, and in the continuance of the rebuilding
of St Peter's his coffin and others from the same chapel (which
was then demolished) were moved to another place, and all
trace of it ultimately lost. In 1913 excavations were begun in

---

[1] The nature of his illness has never been ascertained.

[2] There are two of these in existence. One, written by the secretary
of the Papal Choir, runs thus: 'At midnight Palestrina was carried
into the church (St Peter's), accompanied not only by all the musicians
of Rome, but also by a multitude of people, and according to our
custom we sang the response 'Libera me.' (This was apparently
Palestrina's own music.) The other account is mentioned above.

75

the hope of discovering the composer's remains, but without success. So, with Bach and Mozart, he shares the distinction of resting in an unknown grave.

There can be no doubt that not only in Rome but in all Italy and other European countries it was realized that with Palestrina's death a great musical genius had passed away.

In the eighties of last century the Palestrinian scholar Haberl discovered in one of the Papal Choir books a eulogy of the composer, together with a brief mention of his funeral, written by a certain Melchior Major (or Mafor), which the latter (who signs his name in the book) apparently wrote only a few years after Palestrina's death. Exactly who the writer was we do not know: he was obviously a musician and probably expressed the views of the musical world generally in his long and glowing panegyric of the composer. Having begun by saying that Palestrina 'flourished in the time of our fathers and was most famous for his liturgical music, both masses and motets,' he goes on to enumerate the dead musician's qualities, as those of

one in whom all melody and modulation resided . . . no one in our times showed such great musical gifts as our Palestrina. I declare him to be the father of music, just as Homer was the father of poetry. . . . He was buried in the basilica with an imposing funeral attended by a great company of musicians and others.

As Do Re Mi Fa Sol La all ascend, so does thy name, O Palestrina, rise upward to the stars.

O inevitable Death, bitter and wicked, O cruel Death, thus to rob the churches and the palaces of sweet sounds, for by striking down Palestrina thou has taken away one who irradiated the church with harmony. And because of him, thou, O Music, rest in peace.

Immediately after the composer's death his son Iginio commenced the task of issuing or arranging for the publication of many works still remaining in manuscript. For this he has somewhat unfairly been held up to contempt as one whose sole thought was to exploit his father's reputation as a composer to his own advantage. Since, however, among the works which Iginio's action brought to light were such masterpieces, for example, as the great eight-part masses *Laudate Dominum* and *Hodie Christus natus est*, one should not be too hard on him. Moreover, it is almost certain that Palestrina, when he felt life drawing to a close, would have charged his son with the duty of bringing out the best, at any rate, of his remaining works. The only criticism one may perhaps make of Iginio is that he evidently determined to make something out of every scrap of material left by his father [1]—including the unfinished revision of the Gradual plainchant—either by publishing it himself or selling it to others. His first act was to bring out the volume of masses the printing of which Palestrina was superintending at the time of his death. Iginio, who, like his father, had a pen capable of turning a neat phrase in dedicating prefaces, prepared for this publication an address to the pope (Clement VIII), in which, after expressing the pious hope that his father was now enjoying 'sweet harmonies in the Kingdom of God,' announced his desire to publish 'in the public interest, those labours of my father, consecrated to the Divine praises, which he continued to the end of his life. In fulfilment of this pious wish, I offer to your Holiness this book begun by him and finished by me. There is much more that I hope to issue, should means allow. . . .'

The hint was not entirely lost on the pope. Iginio shortly afterwards received a grant from the papal treasury of 100 scudi towards any publishing expenses. But he seems to have decided to bring out nothing more on his own account,

[1] The Palestrina article in the earlier editions of Grove speaks of Iginio's 'reckless brutality' in publishing the Mass and the Motet on *Tu es pastor ovium*, simply because, in the writer's view, these were inferior works!

disposing of some masses and madrigals to various persons, by whom they were published between 1594 and 1601,[1] six books of masses being issued from this source. In all probability he had no funds wherewith to publish anything more himself. It is doubtful whether Palestrina left much: the fur business had to be liquidated because, according to the custom mentioned in the case of Angelo, the composer's widow was entitled to the return of her dowry. Iginio had a family to maintain, and apparently his only means of earning a livelihood was in the legal profession, for he was a qualified doctor of law.

But the affair of the unfinished Gradual certainly does not do Iginio credit. Some months before his death Palestrina had been approached by a certain Franciscan monk belonging to the Vatican press, Brother Adrian, who with some others had devised a new kind of type for printing the plainchant notation. The suggestion was that Palestrina's work should be completed and the permission of the authorities obtained to issue it in the new type, as the official revised edition of the Gradual plainchant. The composer was offered a handsome sum of money should the project be approved. Palestrina agreed to the scheme and had apparently taken up the work, laid aside some years previously, when death intervened.

It was now Iginio's ambition to carry the matter through and obtain the money promised to his father. The first thing he did was to obtain possession of that portion of the plainchant entrusted to Zoilo, who had died in 1592, and the next to arrange for this and his father's work to be completed by a

[1] The names of two of these purchasers appear on some editions: T. de Argentis and A. de Agnetis. Raugel describes them as 'amateurs,' whatever that may mean. The similarity of the two names suggests that they may have been one and the same person; the view expressed by Cametti is that they were two brothers, 'Agnetis' being merely a printer's error for 'Argentis.'

hack musician. A contract was signed between himself and the other persons concerned, the payment to Iginio being, naturally, dependent on the scheme being successful. The next step was to approach the authorities with the completed Gradual, which Iginio no doubt represented as entirely the work of his father and Zoilo.[1]   Cardinal del Monte, who had charge of such matters, promptly referred it to a committee of musicians for an expert opinion on the value of the revision. The committee, which had evidently got wind of the affair, reported that the Gradual was undoubtedly not the complete work of Palestrina, and was, in fact, full of errors. One must not take their verdict too seriously. There was still in Rome a very strong feeling against any such revision of the ancient plainchant; moreover, one of the committee, a certain Nanino, is reported to have remarked: 'I consider Palestrina to have been a good practical musician, but not of the first, the second or even the third rank' (!).

On the strength of the committee's report, the church authorities refused to proceed any farther. Thereupon Iginio endeavoured to enforce some payment from the other parties and took the matter to court. Proceedings dragged on for several years, and finally the contract between the parties was rescinded and the music ordered to be returned to Iginio. He refused to receive it back and so Palestrina's manuscript, together with Zoilo's and the spurious additions, was sent to the Monte di Pietà, where it remained until lost sight of.

Much of Palestrina's best work still remained unpublished after Iginio had disposed of such manuscripts as his father had left. More existed in the choir-books of St Peter's and the other Roman basilicas, and perhaps elsewhere. Of all this material the authorities concerned apparently refused in most

[1] Or he may have pretended that Palestrina had finished Zoilo's part.

cases to allow the publication, and thus a great deal of Palestrina's finest work remained unknown until early in the nineteenth century, when a first attempt at a collected edition was made in Italy by Abbate Alfieri, who brought out, about 1842, several volumes of masses, motets, magnificats, etc. A little later Proske began to print a number of pieces in his *Musica sacra* (*c.* 1850); then such enthusiastic scholars as de Witt, Commer, Espagne and finally Haberl began those labours which culminated in the great collected edition of the composer's music issued by Breitkopf & Härtel from 1862 to 1907.

CHAPTER VIII

CHARACTERISTICS OF PALESTRINA'S STYLE

MUSIC, like everything else in this world, is subject, in some degree, to the laws of fashion. Even Bach and Beethoven clothed their thoughts mainly in the musical dress of their own day; it is the quality of their ideas and their craftsmanship which has differentiated their work from that of their lesser contemporaries in a similar style. One has only to compare a Bach fugue with a similar work by a contemporary such as G. P. Telemann, or a Beethoven sonata with one by Hummel, whose music was even more fashionable at one time in Vienna than the former's, to realize this fact.

Palestrina's music has that ageless quality which is one of the hall-marks of great art, but externally it belongs unmistakably to its own day, to what is rather loosely termed the 'polyphonic school.' Yet this musical speech is indissolubly bound up with his artistic purpose, since the sixteenth-century polyphony chiefly grew from liturgical soil, and it is an inability to understand the artistic purpose underlying such a style which, for instance, caused Saint-Saëns, in one of his *Outspoken Essays*, to ask the question: 'Wherein does the Kyrie of the famous *Missa Papae Marcelli* express supplication? Here there is nothing else but form.' [1]

[1] On the other hand, Debussy regarded the nineteenth-century 'emotional' liturgical music, such as that written by Gounod, as 'hysteria.'

Judged by the conventional nineteenth-century standard, there is, of course, nothing of emotional expression in this or any other of the ninety-three 'Kyries' Palestrina composed. Mendelssohn shows a similar misunderstanding and the same stereotyped outlook of his day when he complains of Palestrina's 'wasting' beautiful music on the introductory sentence, 'Incipit lamentatio,' and on the titles of chapter or verse in the *Lamentations*, not realizing that this is just as artistically legitimate as the instrumental overture and interludes in a cantata or oratorio, of which indeed such music took the place. In each case the functional idea is the same—to create an appropriate atmosphere in the minds of the hearers, thus calling attention to what is to follow. Mendelssohn admits that some such explanation was furnished, even at that time, in a little book he obtained during Holy Week in Rome, but he still refused to believe in its artistic truth. Even Wagner was not un-influenced by this view of his own times as to what constituted 'expression' in music.[1] We have an example of this in his own edition of Palestrina's *Stabat Mater*, where he has over-loaded the score with incessant dynamic marks, especially in the employment of such essentially nineteenth-century devices as the *crescendo* and the *diminuendo*, instead of allowing the formal patterning of the music, which constitutes its chief beauty, to make its own effect, with, at the most, only a sparing use of a *forte* or a *piano*.[2]

Palestrina's liturgical music neither represents the composer's

[1] Burney, in his *History of Music*, quotes what he amusingly terms an 'attempt at expression' in one of Palestrina's madrigals.

[2] The remarks of the French scholar Choron (1771–1834) on the performance of Palestrina deserve quotation. He says: 'Cette musique doit être chantée en sons filés et soutenus, avec beaucoup de justesse, d'un mouvement égal et modéré, avec la plus grande simplicité.'

personal reaction to the emotional idea of the sacred texts nor provides a 'ready-made' emotion for the listener. It has a rarer quality, its aim being to evoke and develop the requisite mood in the worshipper. Beethoven, it may be remembered, enunciated the same idea in connection with his own Mass, the music of which was primarily meant, he says, 'to awaken and render lasting religious feeling.' Hence in a 'Kyrie' by Palestrina the music is not intended to do more than continually direct the attention and the mind of the hearer to the idea of supplication set forth by the words: this is achieved by the continuous weaving of beautiful and significant lines of tone entwined about the text and framing it. It is, in fact, an appeal, through the ear, to remind the congregation of the significance and meaning of the liturgical act of worship. Palestrina's religious music is to be taken in the same spirit as the work of those medieval architects who built the great churches and the master-craftsmen who fashioned lovely ornaments for them, and it may be regarded, in this way, as merely a receptacle for the sacred text upon which all the art of the musical craftsman has been lavished for its adornment. All is intended to aid corporate worship: thus the music was composed as part of the services, not *for* them. It is this impersonal quality, this aloofness from the human element which gives to such music its mystic atmosphere, its sense of remoteness, of something time-less and ageless, ideal qualities from the liturgical point of view.

The fundamental principle upon which the musical style of Palestrina is based is the decorative one, and it is to be found in plainchant itself. Debussy, whose intensive study of sixteenth-century music has already been referred to, puts the matter admirably (in one of his *Monsieur Croche* articles). Speaking of 'that musical arabesque or rather principle of ornament[1] which is the basis of all forms of art,' he goes on to say:

The primitives, Palestrina, Orlande de Lassus and others, made use of this divine arabesque: they discovered the principle in the Gregorian chant; and they strengthened these delicate traceries by strong counterpoint. It is not the character of the melody which moves us but rather the tracing of a particular line, often indeed of several lines whose meeting, whether by chance or design, makes the appeal.

Debussy had more to say on the same subject in a letter to a friend. He continues:

I consider it a marvellous *tour de force*, those effects which they [the sixteenth-century composers] obtain purely from a profound knowledge [*un science énorme*] of counterpoint—that counterpoint which, as one knows, can be the most crabbed thing [*la chose la plus rébarbative*] in all music. But with them it becomes something to admire, for it underlines the sentiment of the words in a deeply impressive manner: then at times the curvings of the melody remind one of the decorations in an old missal.

Within this essentially formal and decorative scheme Palestrina wrote music which shows a wonderful flexibility and freedom in its melodic lines—diverging, converging, crossing, running parallel, imitating, echoing, at times elaborate, at other times simple, even almost coming to rest in homophonic (note against note) passages whose broad effects seem to foreshadow the later method of using 'vertical' effects of harmony. Sometimes the decoration expands into big, sweeping outlines that give the music an 'architectural' quality. Although as ingenious a contrapuntist as any of his contemporaries, he always subordinated the use of scholastic devices such as canon or fugue to the considerations of beauty of musical effect. And as we shall see in the chapters devoted to the detailed study of his

[1] This word, as Debussy explains, is, of course, not used in the same sense as when employed in text-books on musical notation.

works, he was continually striving towards a greater clarity of style, eliminating redundancies and endeavouring to achieve his effects by comparatively simple means.

This decorative principle in itself contains a certain expressive element, obtained by intensifying or decreasing the decoration. It is to be observed in plainchant; compare, for example, the 'Kyrie' and 'Sanctus' of the festal Mass *Kyrie fons bonitatis*, with the similar movements in the Lenten Mass *Deus Genitor alme*.

The former have rich, elaborate contours:

which contrast strongly with the simple, almost severe, lines of the latter:

We can see the same idea at work in Palestrina's masses, as this comparison between the 'Kyrie' of the Mass *Laudate Dominum* in eight parts, with its strong, brilliant lines:

with the simple one in the *Missa quarta* will show:

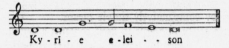

Ky - ri - e   e - lei - - son

Another element of expression in the decorative style is the employment of simple pictorial effects. Naturally Palestrina has not been able to make much use of this in the masses, but there are one or two opportunities of which he has sometimes availed himself. He and his contemporaries seem to have found it hard to set such words as 'descendit de coelis' except to a descending figure, or 'ascendit in coelum' to anything but a *motif* of rising notes. But the motets and madrigals obviously offered more scope for this kind of thing, and accordingly we find a great deal of pictorial patterning in their decorative schemes, if the text invites it. Some illus-trations of this will be found in the chapter devoted to these classes of Palestrina's compositions.

It is interesting to trace a system of variation in the decorative principle as shown in a considerable proportion of Palestrina's masses. The first 'Kyrie eleison' is generally set in bold lines, sometimes of fairly elaborate character. For the 'Christe eleison' a more suave contour may often be observed, and the final 'Kyrie,' while returning to the bolder style of the first, is usually more restrained in movement. Following the symbolic meaning of the liturgical text, this musical differentiation is, of course, intended to signify the distinguishing of the three Persons of the Trinity.

The 'Gloria,' as befits a hymn of praise, is mostly carried out in simple, broad lines, the movement being frequently in step-by-step and note-against-note, resulting in homophonic passages that at times give almost the harmonic effect of a later period. The 'Credo' is also carried out in broad, flowing lines, suitable to a profession of faith; here the decorative style is mostly concerned with producing majestic and dignified effects, in accordance with the enunciation of dogma, the central climax of the movement, the 'Crucifixus,' receiving special treatment in quiet, restrained lines.

In the 'Sanctus' the contrapuntal texture is usually of a flowing, delicate character, and we may often notice a marked 'up and down' movement. It has been suggested that this typifies prayers and incense ascending to heaven, and the praises of the heavenly host descending to join those of the worshippers.

Generally speaking the 'Benedictus' will repeat something of the style of the 'Christe eleison' in its quiet, gentle movement, and in the 'Agnus Dei' the tracery is often more delicate in character than in any other movement of the mass. In the last part of this movement, terminating with the prayer for peace, 'dona nobis pacem,' the polyphony assumes an elaborate character and includes some ingenious canonic resolutions, one or two extra parts being usually added to the original number.

To appreciate the salient technical characteristics of Palestrina's style it is necessary, of course, to dismiss from the mind any idea of a fixed bass supporting definite harmonies and of a melodic idea predominating from time to time. In the combination of vocal lines which his music represents, all are more or less of equal importance in the tonal tissue. Palestrina, indeed, is said to have remarked that he did not mind which voice sang a certain line in some of his works. This is doubtless true in some instances, where perhaps the soprano and tenor, or the second soprano and second tenor, might exchange parts without impairing the general effect of the music.

These vocal lines are woven within the simplest harmonic system, practically the triad and its first inversion; variety is achieved by the use of passing notes, giving to the music a delicate harmonic tinting especially by means of the dissonances ('tensions' as Jeppesen terms them) which often result from their employment. Yet with these simple means Palestrina has not only achieved a surprising variety of effect, but also produced much music of exquisite charm and beauty.

Such passages as this, from the 'Credo' of the *Sine nomine* Mass in four voices (from Book II published in 1567):

and this, from the beautiful *Missa primi toni*:

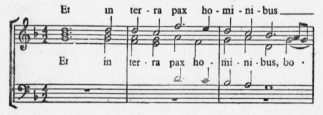

are typical examples among innumerable others to be found throughout the masses and motets, where the simplicity and purity of the harmonies, combined with the delicate tonal flavouring resulting from the passing notes, and the plainchant style of the melodic outlines, produce that mystic, remote feeling so completely appropriate to liturgical music.

When Palestrina (about the time he wrote the *Papae Marcelli* Mass) began to develop his style, a tendency to homophonic writing assumed greater prominence in his music. For this, as we shall see, he was looked at askance by some of his contemporaries, not because they regarded him as an innovator —on the contrary, as reverting to a more primitive style, when counterpoint was actually note against note. (A later age viewed the matter differently, but just as incorrectly, by calling him 'the father of harmony'). Palestrina himself, of course, realized the greater variety to be obtained by employing both decorative polyphony and homophony, the latter providing points of semi-repose contrasting with the movement of the former. A striking illustration of his development of the homophonic style is to be found in the *Stabat Mater* for eight voices (two choirs of four voices each), which was almost certainly written during the last few years of his life. Here the decorative element is very sparingly employed, while on the other hand passages of the homophonic type predominate. The harmonic simplicity of the opening of this magnificent work amazes us just as much as does the wonderful effect produced by a succession of simple triads in root position, sixteen of them consecutively, fourteen major and two minor: the passage is worth quoting if only to show what genius can do with the most elementary material:

The exquisite rhythm of the passage, with its subtle fluctuations, will not escape attention. To confine it within a rigid structure of bars is to spoil its delicate metre.[1]

[1] To what absurdities of rhythm the barring of such music can lead is shown by such an example as this, from the Mass *O magnum mysterium*:

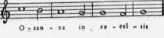

Palestrina's music is written upon the old ecclesiastical modal scales[1] used in his day, and in common with the custom of the period it does not employ bar-lines. It is unhampered by the rigid metre imposed by their use and has something of the free accents and the subtle rhythmic flow of plainchant, only marking, like the latter, the beginning and ending of the musical sentences. The elasticity, resulting from this ability to alter at will the rhythmic tension by compression or elongation, is a freedom Palestrina perpetually employs. It gives to the music a wonderful richness of texture as well as variety and vitality. Striking instances of this rhythmic variation occur in abundance in most of Palestrina's works. We may distinguish two methods in its use—the first where the theme or phrase is immediately repeated in altered form by the same part, the second where it passes with new rhythm to another part, the two variations sometimes overlapping. The employment of the former method is often particularly subtle and ingenious. Here, for example, are illustrations taken from the Mass *Lauda Sion*. The first occurs in the soprano part of the 'Agnus Dei':

[1] It may be remarked, however, that a distinct tendency towards the modern diatonic scale is to be observed in much of Palestrina's music, although some modern editions go too far in their application of the *musica ficta* principle. It was this tendency which perhaps confused Burney (see p. 72).

and almost simultaneously the tenor part shows this further
independent variation:

The repetition of a sub-motive (within the main theme) may
also be noted in both examples, at (*a*) and (*b*), a further instance
of the subtlety of Palestrina's decorative work.

Another striking example, pointed out by Fellerer (in his
Der Palestrinastil), is to be found in the *Sine nomine* Mass (of
Book II), where the 'Kyrie' shows these variants:

The opening of the 'Kyrie' in the *Papae Marcelli* Mass
furnishes an admirable example of the second type of varying
rhythmic tension; the theme passes in succession (at a half-
measure's distance only) from first tenor to soprano, then to
first bass and alto (*see foot of opposite page*).

Palestrina's subtle and beautiful use of the dissonance produced by the clashing of two (sometimes three) contrapuntal
melodies has been exhaustively analysed from the technical
point of view by Jeppesen,[1] and any lengthy exposition of it
would be out of place here. But it may be said that, like the
rhythmic variation, this use of dissonance constitutes another of
the charms of Palestrina's music to the ear.

These dissonances are not, of course, accidental happenings,
arising out of the contrapuntal movements, but carefully
calculated effects, thought out and deliberately introduced for
definite aesthetic reasons. One could not for one moment

[1] *The Style of Palestrina and the Dissonance.*

consider such poignant dissonances as one meets from time to time to be mere contrapuntal accidents, because any well-trained student could have shown Palestrina how to avoid it. When we examine the dissonance in relation to the musical context, it will be seen how the whole passage is designed to lead up to it, as an illumination of the text to which it belongs. Even more remarkable is a passage in the 'Credo' of the Mass *Jesu, nostra redemptio* (the *Missa tertia* of the fourth book), typical of many in Palestrina's work, where one feels that the composer's musical vision has reached to the distant future. This would not have sounded out of place in a mass written more than two centuries later:

The remarkable succession of dissonances (by suspending the fourth) culminating in a double dissonance (marked with a cross) creates an effect no doubt intended to direct the attention of the listener to the recital that follows—of the mysteries of the Incarnation and Passion.

Another striking double dissonance, where, as in the previous example, Palestrina seems to foreshadow modern harmonic methods, is to be found in the 'Christe eleison' of the Mass *Aeterna Christi munera*:

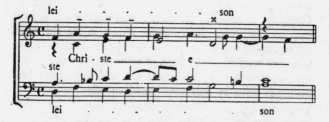

Innumerable other instances of this use of the dissonance as a means of drawing attention to the emotional significance of the text might be quoted, but one final example will suffice—

this phrase from the madrigal *Alla riva del Tebro*, where the pungent dissonances are suggested by the words 'acerba e rea' ('sour and evil'):

The secular madrigals, indeed, have many remarkable passages of this nature.

The extent to which Palestrina's liturgical music is based upon the plainchant has already been mentioned. It is hardly an exaggeration to say that the greater part of it owes its origin to this source, and that without plainchant we should never have had the greatest of his music.

As far as the masses are concerned their titles in many cases proclaim a derivation of this kind: it is the same in the case of the motets, much of their music being built upon the corresponding plainchant settings of the text, taken from the Gradual. Even where the themes seem more or less original, they are cast in the same mould, always in the old modal scales, and reflecting the spirit of the plainchant in their contours and rhythms. There are, of course, exceptions; some of the masses were composed upon secular themes, taken from madrigals either by Palestrina himself or other composers: in a few instances he apparently borrowed thematic ideas from motets written by various musicians. But the bulk of his religious music is, of course, inspired by the plainchant which indeed permeates its fabric, being part of the very weave, spun out of the 'germ' ideas provided by the original themes, the counterpoints deriving from them by means of the decorative principle with its rhythmic and melodic line variation. The Palestrinian method, in fact, may in some respects be compared to the symphonic structure of two centuries later.

But themes were not all-important to Palestrina, which is perhaps the reason why he invented so few for himself. The contours of an already existing theme and its association with a particular idea were sufficient to act as a stimulus and set in motion that inexhaustible flow of polyphony of which he possessed the gift. In his finest works, indeed, the themes are often only vaguely recognizable, buried in the substructure of the movements, and we feel that they are only of secondary importance, compared with the effects produced by their means.

Reference has been made to Palestrina's employment of the *Leitmotiv* system. Its use was evidently suggested to him by plainchant, in which a primitive form of the idea may be traced—a decorative figure recurring (sometimes in modified shape) from time to time and often identifiable with a particular idea. Palestrina began by adopting the principle as he found it in plainsong, but subsequently subjected it to development on his own account. We can observe this best in the masses, where the large-scale movements, connected liturgically, obviously offered most scope for the employment of such a system. Examples of such development will be found in the following chapter (on the music of the masses), where we shall find representative themes assigned to each Person of the Trinity, set forth in the three sections of the 'Kyrie' and reappearing in the later movements, whenever the text invites such thematic reference. And in their passage from movement to movement these themes undergo modification in accordance with a definite aesthetic design. Other representative themes will usually be added as the work proceeds—a *motif* of praise for

97

the 'Gloria,' an 'ascension' figure in the 'Credo' and so forth.

No survey, however brief, of Palestrina's musical style would be complete without some consideration of his music from the purely choral standpoint. In all his works he displays a complete mastery and knowledge of the effects obtainable in vocal tone-colour, and the subtlety and variety he achieves is remarkable. One might describe it as choral scoring. He knows, for example, how to produce a piece in brilliant colours for festal use or how to give sober hues to music written around words expressive of sorrow or suffering. Such effects and many others are obtained by the grouping together of various voices, by combination, by contrast and by the use of the different registers; the method is perhaps best observable in works written for five or six parts (rather than in those for eight parts, where the effect is often that of two choirs, each of four parts, used antiphonally).

In some of the more elaborate works there is a constant grouping and regrouping, contrasting and combining the voices—in twos, threes, fours, fives and sixes, exhausting in turn all the possible permutations and combinations—the changes going on swiftly and continuously, giving almost a kaleidoscopic effect. Thus at one moment the tonal tissue may be carried on by first and second soprano and first tenor, the next moment continued by first and second tenors and second bass, followed by alto and second tenor, then by soprano, alto, first tenor and first and second basses, and so on.

At times one part alone may be thrown into momentary prominence against a background provided by some or all of the others, as, for example, in the 'Sanctus' of the *Papae Marcelli* Mass, where the sopranos begin with a melody against sustained phrases for alto, second tenor and second bass, thus:

PALESTRINA'S MUSICAL AUTOGRAPH

*A page from the famous Codex 59 (in the archives of St. John Lateran)
containing the only known manuscripts in the composer's own hand*

We may note, too, how the choice of voices is made according to the style of the work. In the *Papae Marcelli* Mass, for example, the six parts are for soprano, alto, first and second tenor, first and second bass, giving the somewhat dark tonal hues appropriate to this music, dignified almost to the point of austerity, while for the six-part *Assumpta est Maria* the voices are first and second sopranos, alto, first and second tenors and bass, affording opportunity for brilliant yet delicate colouring. It has been

99

pointed out by more than one writer that in music written in honour of the Blessed Virgin—to whom Palestrina seems to have had a particular devotion—the voices are always disposed so as to produce a special sweetness and purity of effect, as well as a delicate radiance. For example, in the opening of the motet for the Feast of the Assumption, Palestrina employs two sopranos and the upper register of the first tenor to produce an exquisite clarity and brilliance of tone:

Other examples of this are the motets *Ave Maria* (from the book of offertories), the *Salve Regina* (in five parts), the *Ave*

Regina coelorum, Alma Redemptoris and many others of a similar type, all of which have been described as 'shining with a mystical radiance.'

In a good many of the masses one finds a definite scheme of tone-colour—the bright-toned first part of the 'Credo,' contrasting with the soft-hued 'Incarnatus'; the glowing colouring of the 'Christe eleison,' the even more delicate tinting of the 'Benedictus' (suggestive of the Celestial Visitant), the brilliant, yet diaphanous, web of sound in the 'Sanctus' and the rich, soft colour of the 'Agnus Dei.'

CHAPTER IX

THE MASSES

IT is in his masses that Palestrina's genius soars to its highest point, in their music most of all that he has realized his ideal as a musical creator—music in which his faith and art were fused together into one supreme act of adoration for the Holy Sacrifice.

The word 'mass' is here intended to signify what is termed in the Roman Catholic liturgy the Ordinary of the Mass, i.e. the sung part of the mass which is invariable—the 'Kyrie,' 'Gloria,' 'Credo,' 'Sanctus,' 'Agnus Dei,' as distinct from the rest of the sung liturgy known as the 'Proper,' comprising Introit, Gradual (sometimes with 'Alleluia' and Tract or Sequence), Offertorium and Communio, all of which vary from day to day.

Palestrina wrote more than ninety masses. The number is usually given as ninety-three [1] (thirty-nine in four parts, twenty-eight in five parts, twenty-two in six parts and four in eight parts). In such a quantity (less, however, than one-third the total amount of his work) the quality must necessarily vary; but generally speaking these masses show a high level of musical beauty and workmanship which is really astounding and without a parallel elsewhere, unless it be the church cantatas of Bach. One writer (Félix Raugel) has described them as 'un ensemble de chefs-d'œuvre,' and although this must, of

[1] The Breitkopf & Härtel edition prints ninety-four: one or two are of doubtful authenticity.

FROM THE SECOND BOOK OF MASSES (1567)

The picture shows the style of music-printing in Palestrina's day and the beautiful woodcuts to be found on every page. As this example is from a mass in honour of the Blessed Virgin ('Missa Inviolata') the picture shows her with the Infant Jesus

course, be considered as an enthusiastic exaggeration, one can at least say that a large proportion of them are certainly master-pieces, while on the other hand only a very few can be considered as inferior, dull or uninspired works. Perhaps their most remarkable feature is the diversity of style they show: each has an individual character; we seldom find Palestrina repeating time after time any particular turn of phrase or type of development—a remarkable thing when one remembers the limited system in which he worked. But he achieved variety of effect, not only by employing a wide range of musical subjects, but also, as already pointed out, by an apparently inexhaustible resource in contrapuntal writing and a consummate skill in the use of the voices.

In the polyphonic period the mass held that position of importance, musically, which in later times was assigned to the symphony. Palestrina's masses, indeed, have been termed vocal symphonies; but in some cases, especially in the works of smaller calibre, perhaps a juster comparison would be with chamber music. In such a mass, for example, as the *Aeterna Christi munera*, in four parts, we shall find music where the purity, delicacy and balance of the part-writing suggests that of a string quartet.

Any detailed consideration of the masses would obviously be impossible within the limits of this volume, and therefore only certain representative works can be chosen for analysis and as illustrations of the composer's achievement in this field.

The masses may be classified not only according to their musical but also their liturgical style. As far as the latter category is concerned they can be grouped into two divisions: those for ordinary use (usually in four parts only), comparatively short and simple in style, and those for special occasions, feast-days and ceremonies, which are longer and more elaborate.

In both classes are to be found masterpieces—in the former such exquisite little masses as the *Jesu, nostra redemptio, Iste confessor, Brevis* and the *Sine nomine* (of Book II); in the latter such magnificent works as the *Dum complerentur, Hodie Christus* and *Assumpta est.*

The division into musical styles is not so easy, as Palestrina was apparently in the habit of constantly working over earlier material. He and his son Iginio were responsible for the publication of thirteen books of his masses: of these six appeared during his lifetime, death overtaking him while superintending the publication of the seventh. Eighty masses were printed in these thirteen books; most of the thirteen others seem to have remained unpublished until collected editions of Palestrina's music began to appear.

In the thirteen books mentioned both early and later works often appear side by side: for example, in the third volume, of 1570, we find the early five-part mass on the theme of the song *L'homme armé*, and the *Missa brevis* written perhaps fifteen years later; in the fourth book (1582), *Jesu, nostra redemptio*, probably composed about 1575, and the four-part *L'homme armé*, which dates from a still earlier period; in the fifth book (1590), late works such as *Aeterna Christi munera* and *Iste confessor* are to be found with the work composed on the madrigal *Nasce la gioja mia*; in the ninth book (1599), the great *Missa Te Deum laudamus*, which was certainly composed in the last years of Palestrina's life, is beside an early mass based upon the madrigal *Vestiva i colli*. (The madrigal itself was probably written about 1560: it appears, with a lute accompaniment, in a collection issued in 1568 by Vincenzo Galileo, father of the astronomer.) So it seems quite probable that it was Palestrina's custom to work simultaneously at new compositions and the revision of earlier ones, selecting from both if he was about to issue a new book.

However, a consideration of the musical style of the masses themselves suggests that we may divide them roughly into three periods: the first of these would comprise those written or commenced up to the time when Palestrina left St Agapit's for Rome, in which the style and influence of the Franco-Flemish school is prominent. A totally new manner was inaugurated with the well-known *Missa Papae Marcelli*; even among other works written about the same time it stands out distinct and individual, especially because of its remarkable dignity and austerity of style. We then come to a period when a melodic suavity began to give the contrapuntal texture a new richness and beauty. Outstanding examples of this are the *Aeterna Christi munera*, the *Iste confessor* and the *Assumpta est*. The end of this period saw a final flowering of Palestrina's genius, during the last few years of his life, in such 'architectural' masterpieces as the eight-part *Laudate Dominum*, the six-part *Te Deum laudamus* and *Ecce ego Joannes*.

Not a great deal need be said about the masses of the first period. They comprise those of the first book, which have already been mentioned, printed in 1554, and others that were issued at various times, either revised or left untouched. It is fairly safe to assign the composition of those with secular titles to this first period, or the beginning of the second period, since it is quite unlikely that Palestrina would have chosen such themes after the strongly expressed opinion of the Tridentine Council in 1563, and he may even have made such a rule for himself after the memorable address of Pope Marcellus II to the Papal Choir in 1555.

Some of these masses appear in disguised form, others with the original secular title attached (as, for example, the first of the two composed on the theme of the old song *L'homme armé*). Among those which obviously belong to the earlier period, their music showing unmistakably the Franco-Flemish influence, are, in addition to the work just mentioned, those entitled *Repleatur os meum* and *De beata Virgine*; the Hexachord Mass, (*Ut, Re, Mi, Fa, Sol, La*), *Ad fugam* and *Primi toni* (upon the theme of Ferrabosco's madrigal *Io mi son giovinetta*). The first four works mentioned appeared in the 1570 book, and according to Cametti one reason for their publication was that already criticism had been directed against Palestrina for his new style, which was declared to 'show more fantasy than learning.' It was also said that he preferred writing in the easier homophonic style to using elaborate polyphony. Palestrina therefore replied to the charge by printing these brilliant essays in the FrancoFlemish style, dating back perhaps fifteen to twenty years,[1] in which he shows a command of contrapuntal science equalling that of the most distinguished representatives of that school. The Mass *Repleatur os meum*, for example, treats the principal theme in canon at the octave in the 'Kyrie,' at the seventh in the 'Christe,' at the sixth in the second 'Kyrie,' at the fifth in the 'Gloria,' at the fourth in the 'Credo,' at the third in the 'Sanctus' and at the second in the 'Hosanna,' while the 'Agnus Dei' treats it in unison, with the subject in augmentation, the second part giving two resolutions at different intervals! As a specimen of ingenuity it is unrivalled.[2]

The first important work of this early period is the *Ecce sacerdos magnus*, of which some account has already been given. In it we find all the characteristics of the popular style of the period. It is written around a *canto fermo*, the fine melody of the vespers antiphon for a popeconfessor, which constantly recurs, in each part, without variation, and with the original

---

[1] The Hexachord Mass, for instance, was copied into the Papal Choir books in 1562, and evidently composed even before that date.

[2] Raugel suggests that its title might well be 'Mass in Canon at every interval.'

words attached to it (one of the things the Tridentine Council rightly wished to suppress). Around it are counterpoints, either independent or derived from the theme itself.

Ec - ce sa - cer-dos mag-nus qui in di - eb - us su - is

pla-cu - it De - o et in - vent us est just - us

This scheme, typical of the northern school of composition, is carried out with the usual ingenuity.

As a young man Palestrina followed the general musical custom of showing brilliance as a composer by taking themes previously utilized by others and endeavouring to give them a new treatment. Two instances which may be quoted are the five-part mass, just mentioned, on the melody of the old song *L'homme armé*, and the Hexachord (*Ut, Re, Mi,* etc.) Mass in six parts. *L'homme armé*, which seems to have been a French ditty of the thirteenth century, was a favourite theme for both French and Flemish composers; at the time Palestrina was writing his own work, there were already in existence nearly a score of masses upon the same subject, including examples by Josquin des Prés, Pierre de la Rue and the Spanish composer Morales. There was nothing unusual in Palestrina's adding to the number: themes were considered common property in those days, even original ones being freely borrowed. There were also a number of masses constructed on the hexachord which were known to Palestrina before he wrote his own example.

Both works show by their style that they belong to the early period. As in the case of the *Ecce sacerdos magnus*, we find the *canto fermo* appearing from time to time in its original form, in long notes (usually the breve) in the midst of the polyphonic weaving. In the 'Adoramus te' of the 'Gloria' in *L'homme armé* it is so augmented that each of the first two notes of the theme is prolonged for nine breves, forming, in fact, a species of internal 'pedal,' thus:

The Hexachord Mass is equally elaborate; the polyphony in the 'Sanctus,' a maze of scales ascending and descending, passing from one to another of the six voices, makes an especially fine effect, with its lace-like tissue of sound. In the *De beata Virgine*, based upon a plainchant theme, a textual interpolation of some words used in the masses for feasts of the Blessed Virgin [1] was originally to be found in the 'Gloria,' a proof of the early origin of the work.

With the *Missa Papae Marcelli* Palestrina inaugurated a new style, the ultimate development of which was to lead to such

---

[1] These words were deleted from the missal by Pope Pius V in the same year in which this mass was published.

perfect works as the *Aeterna Christi munera, Iste confessor, Assumpta est* and others which represent the height of his powers so far as the mass is concerned.

The probable origin of the *Papae Marcelli* has already been discussed. Pope Marcellus, on that memorable Good Friday, expressed views which Palestrina had doubtless already formu-lated for himself: that the greater art would come from the truer serving of the liturgical needs; that the tendency to over-elaborate and over-ornament, unnecessary complexity and the undue repetition of words (even of syllables), the use of inter-polated themes with their original texts—all these things must give place to a purer style which might well take for its musical maxim the words of the pope: 'Audiri atque percipi.'

And so in this work, the first of the great Palestrinian master-pieces, the older method with its *canto fermo* (or principal theme) and its displays of contrapuntal cleverness merely for the exhibition and exercise of ingenuity has gone. In its place is a logical scheme, a weaving of the polyphonic strands from certain 'germ' themes, artistic effect being achieved by the use of a more restrained type of decoration in the counterpoints, by the balancing of the latter, in combination and in contrast, giving each part equal importance and independence (instead of centring them all around a *canto fermo*) and by the more skilful and subtle use of vocal colour. Subsequent experience, however, led Palestrina to modify something of the angularity and austerity which the music, in spite of its greatness, possesses.

But the *Papae Marcelli* Mass, although by no means Palestrina's finest (as is sometimes claimed for it by many writers), is never-theless one of the first rank. Its most striking features are its perfect proportions, architectural in design, its remote atmosphere and its remarkable dignity, at times almost approaching austerity, while liturgically it conforms to the maxims laid down by Pope Marcellus, of simplicity, clarity and intelligibility of words.

The music probably took some years to complete. It may have been begun in 1555, but in all probability it was laid aside owing to external events—Palestrina's dismissal from the Papal Choir and the troubled, difficult times in which Rome found itself owing to war. Possibly work upon it was not resumed until after the composer had settled down in his new post at St John Lateran, about the beginning of 1556. The mass was in all probability completed by the time he left that church (in August 1560), for the music is to be found in the Papal Choir books a year or so after that date.

In an elaborate and minute analysis of the *Missa Iste confessor* Michael Haller has shown how the beautiful melody of the hymn (belonging to the vespers for the commemoration of a confessor) has been divided into seven *motifs*, and that these appear, in some form or other, in two-thirds of the total number of measures which the mass contains, while in the remaining third traces of them are to be found. One might describe such a method as a kind of vocal symphonic development, and the *Papae Marcelli* is a first essay in this style, although the various themes upon which it is built have not any common origin, neither are they subjected to such a thorough and exhaustive development as in the mass referred to.

There has been much discussion as to the origin of these themes. Raugel speaks of this mass and others as 'everywhere perfumed with the charm of Gregorian melody,' and such a description is certainly true. Yet on the other hand no one seems to have noticed that one of these principal *motifs*:

is no other than the first phrase of *L'homme armé*.

But it is, in fact, also a plainsong 'germ' which is to be found

in many places, as, for instance, in the 'Alleluia' of the Easter
Mass (*Lux et origo*):

Al-le — — lu ia

and, as Raugel points out, it forms the general outline of the
first 'Kyrie' in the same mass. The tune of the song was quite
obviously modelled on plainsong, and if it were not that
Palestrina seems to have been a person somewhat devoid of
humour, one might have suspected him of choosing this
particular phrase in order to have a sly dig at the Council of
Trent.

This first *motif*, a sturdy pedestal which supports much of
the musical structure, symbolizes the First Person of the Trinity.
At once Palestrina begins to spin contrapuntal threads from
it, as the opening of the stately 'Kyrie' (quoted in the previous
chapter) shows, every one of the six parts being occupied
with the theme in different ways: here and in the rest of the mass
the polyphonic movement is always quiet and dignified. Also
in this 'Kyrie,' and indeed throughout the mass, we may
notice how Palestrina uses the six voices with remarkable
variety of effect, continually regrouping, withdrawing and
re-entering them, in fresh melodic patterns. At the 'Christe'
a simple, undulating little *motif* appears, giving a softer touch
to the musical fabric—a beginning of that more melodious
style of counterpoint which was to flower so beautifully in the
later masses.

The third 'Kyrie' introduces a short theme apparently derived
from the plainsong *Conditor Kyrie omnium*, which appears first in
the lowest voice, and in fuller form in the highest (soprano)
part, thus:

This new theme represents the Third Person of the Trinity; a reference to it occurs, for example, in the 'Credo' at the words 'Et incarnatus est de Spiritu Sancto.' A motif of praise is introduced in the 'Gloria,' at the words 'Laudamus te,' this being easily recognizable as taken from the plainsong mass *Dominator Deus*:

Lau·da·mus te

Its simple but unmistakable outline dominates the opening of this majestic hymn, the earlier themes being introduced from time to time in altered shape and in fragmentary form, especially where the text gives opportunity for such reference, for example, the 'Christe' theme at the words 'filius patris.' The motif of praise is reintroduced with fine effect for the closing Amens.

The 'Credo,' with its sonorous opening phrases founded upon the theme on p. 111, is perhaps the finest movement in the mass. Its big outlines, constantly dominated by the themes quoted above, and the stately movement of the voices together give the music a remarkable nobility and dignity. The central climax is especially fine—the voices all sweeping downward in turn, at the words 'descendit de coelis,' followed by the impressive harmonies of the 'Et incarnatus' which lead to the beautiful 'Crucifixus,' where the six parts are reduced to four: here again the voices mostly move note against note, in phrases of simple but poignant effect.

The stately movement is resumed at 'Et in Spiritum Sanctum Dominum,' its final cadences being a series of rolling Amens, echoed from voice to voice:

In the 'Sanctus' the voices sweep up and down in broad, wavelike movements, solemn and mystic in effect. The 'Benedictus,' where the voices are again reduced to four, is a meditative movement of devotional feeling, its gently flowing counterpoints being largely woven from this fine theme:

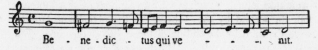

The 'Agnus Dei' brings once more a highly developed polyphonic design, like the earlier movements, on broad, sweeping lines.

The popular *Missa brevis* may have been composed during the same period as the *Papae Marcelli*, or perhaps just after, for although its slighter texture is in contrast with the basilica-like structure of the latter, the two works show some resemblances of style. The popularity of the *Missa brevis* is certainly deserved, for among the four-part masses it occupies a place by itself for beauty of effect as well as ingenious structure. Two statements usually made about this mass seem open to question. The first concerns the title, which is generally supposed to refer to the fact that some of the principal themes begin with the long note known as the breve. However, as so many themes utilized in masses written at this period—some of Palestrina's among them—commence with a similar note, one would hardly imagine this fact to provide a sufficiently distinguishing title. On the other hand the modest dimensions of the movements, especially of the 'Kyrie,' 'Gloria' and 'Credo,' suggest an equally probable origin for the word *brevis*, the movements in question being certainly shorter than the average of those in Palestrinian masses. The second statement is that the themes of this work are taken from a motet, *Audi filia*, by Goudimel. One of them is certainly not derived from that source, the theme of the 'Benedictus,' for it is no other than the little plainchant motif 'Laudamus te' (from the Mass *Dominator Deus*), which, as we have seen, had already been utilized by the composer in the *Papae Marcelli*. And the others seem to reflect in their contours many a fragment of plainchant; in the 'Kyrie' the first theme may have been suggested by a familiar 'Credo' intonation, the second by the 'Christe' of the plainchant *Firmator sancte*, the third by the ending of the eighth psalm tone. But whatever the precise origin of the themes, they give rise to music of much grace and beauty. In the 'Christe eleison' we find a passage typical of many in the later masses—an expressive melody in the tenor part, in counterpoint against the principal theme:

Its flowing phrases, surprisingly modern compared with the general style of the period, shows how Palestrina had already begun to develop that melodic suavity in his counterpoints, in place of the more angular contours of the Franco-Flemish school, which is exhibited to such perfection in a mass like the *Aeterna Christi munera*. The 'Gloria' alternates between a simple homophony and a flowing contrapuntal movement. A good example of the former is the beautiful 'Qui tollis,' upon the 'Christe' theme:

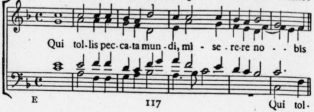

and as illustrating the latter this passage, with its fragment of tenor [1] melody and exquisite cadence, which occurs more than once in the mass:

The 'Credo' has much of the same appealing simplicity as the 'Gloria,' but is less homophonic. A novel and beautiful effect occurs just after the 'Crucifixus,' where, while the soprano and alto parts are still lingering on the words 'sepultus est,' first the bass and then the tenor break in with a vigorous 'et resurrexit,' as if impatient to announce the glad tidings. The whole passage is worth reproducing, as typical of so many fine moments in this mass:

[1] The frequent prominence of the tenor voice whenever there is a textual reference to Our Lord will not escape the attention of those

In the 'Sanctus' the four-note figure of the 'Kyrie' theme is silhouetted against a background of wave-like figures ascending and descending, as in the *Papae Marcelli*, and with equally fine effect. The delicate 'Benedictus,' in three parts, with its concluding 'Hosanna' (in four parts), is one of the finest movements in the mass, but the 'Agnus Dei' is almost equally beautiful, with its lovely soaring phrases at the commencement and the striking passages which follow, upon a diminished version of the principal theme.

Another mass probably belonging to this same period is that entitled *Spem in alium*, published in 1570 with the *Papae Marcelli* and showing some of the characteristics of the same musical style in its quiet, restrained, dignified polyphony, which often gives place to striking passages where a more purely harmonic effect is produced.

Some of the masses which appeared in the fourth book (published in 1581) were probably composed during the years between 1571 and that date and may therefore be considered

who have studied Palestrina's masses. His fondness for this particular voice may also be attributed to the tradition which assigns to him a voice of the same kind.

to represent a transition period leading from the *Papae Marcelli* and its contemporary masses to those of the final period. Two of them may be singled out for special mention—the four-part *Missa prima* and *Missa tertia*, which may be considered as prototypes of the *Aeterna Christi munera* and *Iste confessor*. Like the two latter, they are founded on metrical plainchant as used for office hymns and sequences. The themes of the first are derived from the sequence *Lauda Sion* sung at mass on the feast of Corpus Christi, the other being based upon the vespers hymn of Ascensiontide.

The *Lauda Sion* sequence is of considerable length, and contains a number of *motifs*: only four of them are used in the construction of the mass, these being as follows:

The music of this mass is perhaps most remarkable for the 'solidity' of the writing, the note-against-note style reaching a climax in a number of passages, based upon the 'Bone Pastor' *motif*, where the effect is surprisingly modern in its suggestion of massive harmonies: these alternate with some based upon the other themes and in a more polyphonic style.

In the gently undulating plainchant of the Ascensiontide hymn—called in Palestrina's day *Jesu, nostra redemptio*, but now known as *Salutis humanae Sator*, he found exactly the right type of thematic material for the style he was now developing. The music of this mass (usually known by the title *Jesu, nostra redemptio* instead of its original *Missa tertia*) has a quiet charm which gives it almost the character of a meditation on the Redemption, especially as at every textual mention of the Saviour the music momentarily takes on a new beauty and significance.

The 'Christe eleison,' for example, has a remarkably suave and delicate contrapuntal movement; here and also in the 'Sanctus' and 'Agnus Dei' the closely woven texture of the music gives it a certain emotional intensity. The 'Gloria' and 'Credo' both contain more of the decorative element than simple homophony, and the rhythmic variations are also very striking.

The 'Credo' is almost the finest movement: the beauty and significance of the music from the words 'Deum de Deo' (beginning with a superb passage on an eloquent little *motif* introduced by the tenors) to the end of the 'Crucifixus' again seems as if inspired by the title of the mass. The lovely little phrase of suspensions, at the words 'descendit de coelis,' quoted in the previous chapter, is another of the many beauties to be found in the 'Credo,' and indeed the whole mass abounds in such.

The writing of the Mass *Jesu, nostra redemptio* was to lead to three others, two of them acknowledged masterpieces, all based upon plainchant hymns. These are the *Aeterna Christi munera*, where the themes are taken from the Matins hymn for feasts of Apostles and Evangelists; *Iste confessor*, based upon the vespers hymn for a confessor; and the *Jam Christus astra*, written around the themes of the Matins hymn for Pentecost.

The first of these occupies a unique position among Palestrina's smaller masses. It is a marvel of simplicity, the clarity of the music, the fluent ease and melodic charm of all the four voice parts combining to produce an atmosphere of devotional meditation pervading the entire work. Very noticeable, too, is the tendency of the music towards a feeling for the modern major mode, while the thematic transformation from movement to movement affords another feature of particular interest.

The short four-line hymn has only three *motifs*:

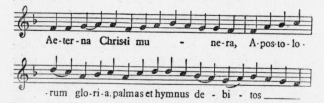

Ae-ter-na Christi mu — ne-ra, A-pos-to-lo-

-rum glo-ri-a. palmas et hymnus de - bi - tos

(the first being repeated for the last line), and these are at once assigned to the first 'Kyrie,' the 'Christe' and the second 'Kyrie' respectively. The second is immediately expanded into a very expressive melody, of which much use is made wherever there is an allusion to the Saviour: here is, for example, an exquisite tenor melody founded upon it in the 'Gloria,' recalling a similar effect in the *Missa brevis*:

u-ni-ge-ni-te, Je - su Chri-ste,

(uni-) ge-ni-te, Je - su Chri - ste Do-mi-ne

Je-su - - Chri - ste,

Je - su Chri - ste, Do-mi-ne

The variation of these simple themes, in each movement, is most ingenious. The 'Christe' *motif* appears in a new form as a long-drawn-out melody in the 'Benedictus,' and the first 'Kyrie' theme is transformed into this pleading phrase at the 'Agnus Dei':

But it is the effect of the music as a whole, rather than of any particular passages, its perfectly balanced phrases and effects, that have justly aroused the admiration of so many musicians, including Wagner.

In the Mass *Iste confessor* we find the same supple, melodious counterpoints that are a characteristic feature of the mass just discussed. Some reference to its elaborate and ingenious construction was made at the beginning of this chapter, and indeed the music presents a particularly interesting study from a technical point of view. For the hymn melody (suave in contour and repeating itself once or twice) is constantly divided into different *motifs*, and occasionally quite a long part of its melodic line appears intact. The result is a very striking musical effect—we feel the constant presence of the melody, yet it is nearly always intangible, dissolved into the musical fabric; the work as a whole gives an impression of meditative charm.

The exquisite little 'Benedictus' especially produces this effect: laid out for alto, first and second bass, the style of the writing, with the bass parts constantly crossing each other, the contrasting of their baritone and lower registers, the intimate blending of all three voices, suggests once again instrumental methods of scoring applied to voices.

A completely contrasted method of treating a plainchant hymn melody is to be found in the six-part *Veni Creator*, composed somewhat earlier than the preceding work, probably during the period 1560-70, although the music was not published in its composer's lifetime, nor indeed for many years after his death.

A remarkable feature of this mass is the instrumental-like form of the movements. Here the melody, instead of being elusive and intangible, is always boldly prominent; it is not divided into separate *motifs* but always used in full in each part of the mass, as if Palestrina had thought—and one may agree with him—that the ear could hardly tire of this most lovely Gregorian tune.

Its treatment often suggests the chorale prelude, especially in the 'Kyrie,' 'Sanctus' and 'Benedictus,' and 'Agnus Dei.' Here the melody appears in long notes in the uppermost (first soprano) part, with counterpoints either of independent origin, or only remotely connected with the melody. Some passages, indeed, are almost Bach-like in style, and might be effectively transcribed for organ.

In the 'Gloria' and 'Credo' the melody, still in the first soprano part, appears in shorter notes and is repeated as required: two 'interludes' separate its repetitions in the 'Gloria,' new material being introduced for the 'Crucifixus' of the 'Credo,' while the 'Veni Creator' melody resumes at the words 'Et in unum Spiritum.'

The important group of masses written upon the antiphons and for the feasts of the Blessed Virgin may fittingly be considered together, as they have some characteristics of style in common, especially a lightness and delicacy of texture, both in design and vocal colour. Some of Palestrina's best music is to be found in them, and also in the similar group of motets in honour of the Blessed Virgin, to whom the composer seems to have had a particular devotion: indeed, in the preface to his fourth book of motets (quoted in Chapter I) he makes reference to this.

This group of masses includes both early and late works—in the former category those in four parts, such as the *Inviolata* and *De beata Virgine* (both published in 1567), the six-part *Ave Maria* (which did not appear in print until 1594) and the six-part *De beata Virgine* (published in 1570, but obviously written much earlier). The masses belonging to a later period include the four-part *Ave Regina coelorum* and *Regina coeli*; the six-part *Assumpta est* and *Alma Redemptoris*, all of which were unpublished at the time of Palestrina's death. In every case these masses are composed upon plainchant themes belonging to the various antiphons whose titles they bear. The finest of them all is the *Assumpta est Maria*, upon the music of which Palestrina seems to have lavished all his art, as a musical tribute to the Mother of God: indeed, it is a work which many critics hold to be his finest in this form.

In any case it must be included in the front rank of his masses. The date at which it was written is uncertain: earlier biographies assert that it was composed in haste for the Feast of the Assumption (15th August) in 1585 and performed on that day at Santa Maria Maggiore. Upon what authority this statement is made does not appear, and as Baini adds that the music was in print by this date (a most obvious error) the story seems improbable. One imagines that the first performance of such a masterpiece would have been reserved either for the Papal Choir or that of St Peter's (Palestrina's own choir). And on the other hand, the music itself bears no trace of being written hastily; on the contrary it shows evidence of that careful working over and polishing up which the composer himself has told us he usually gave to his work. As it was never published in his lifetime, nor included among those sold off by Iginio, we may assume that it was either composed later than 1585 or if begun then (perhaps earlier), not completed and revised until some years later.

The gladness and rejoicing of a great festal day sound through all the music of this mass, which, although elaborately written in six parts, has always a remarkable lightness and delicacy of texture, and at the same time great brilliance and richness. As in the case of the motet bearing a similar title, the particular voices chosen (two sopranos, alto, two tenors, bass) are those most suitable to producing the desired effects: it may be noted how the upper registers of the voices (even of the basses) are continuously employed to obtain as light and brilliant a tone as possible.

There is really only one central theme—the antiphon for Lauds of the feast day:

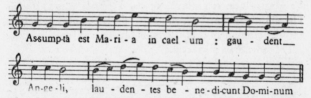

Assump-tà est Ma-ri-a in cael-um : gau-dent—
An-ge-li, lau-den-tes be-ne-di-cunt Do-mi-num

The remaining thematic material consists of fragments evolved from this, or scraps of plainchant; but a little figure of five ascending notes, constantly used decoratively, may perhaps be regarded as a theme symbolical of the Assumption. We meet with it at once in the joyful figures of the 'Kyrie'—for the atmosphere of rejoicing tinges even the prayer for mercy—which soar up and down with beautiful effect. Here and in the other movements the decorative element has an exuberance quite unusual in Palestrina's later works, and we may notice how this decoration is especially luxuriant in the two soprano and two tenor parts, giving a silvery quality to the vocal tone; also it may be pointed out how the parts continually cross and recross each other (especially in the voices just mentioned), giving a diaphanous texture to the musical fabric.

The 'Christe eleison' must be specially mentioned for its unusual style—four voices only are employed: alto, two tenors and bass—giving an effect that might be compared to a move-ment for the lower strings of an orchestra. The hushed phrase with which it opens, the mellow tone and dignified beauty of those which follow, make it one of the most impres-sive moments of the mass. In two other movements where four voices only are employed, we find again a wonderful sense of colour. In the 'Crucifixus' the music is laid out for two sopranos and two altos, the principal theme being divided between the voices; the exquisite 'Benedictus,' a most delicately beautiful piece of decorative counterpoint, is scored (one feels the word is almost justified) for two sopranos, alto and tenor. The short 'Hosanna' which follows the last-named movement, with its combination of the homophonic and polyphonic, is full of radiant joy:

The stately 'Gloria' and 'Credo,' if not so remarkable as the other movements, yet continue the atmosphere of rejoicing with fine effect. Both contain more polyphonic passages than usual.

The two masses (in four and six parts respectively) bearing the title *De beata Virgine* form a most interesting study. Both are written upon the plainsong Mass *Cum jubilo,* one of the two intended for use at feasts of the Blessed Virgin. It would be almost more correct to describe the four-part work as a free arrangement of the plainchant music, since the whole of this is utilized. In the 'Gloria,' for instance, the original plain-chant movement is repeated phrase by phrase, with the voices in close imitation. The 'Kyrie' is merely a more elaborate setting of the plainchant, and the same method is to some extent employed in the 'Sanctus' and 'Agnus Dei.' As no plainchant mass possesses a 'Credo' of its own, Palestrina has utilized the first of the four plainchant 'Credos,' setting it in similar fashion.

The six-part *De beata Virgine* is composed more or less in the same style, but without quite the same rigid adherence to the plainchant movements. In the first 'Agnus Dei,' for example, the theme of the 'Sanctus' is repeated, and the 'Credo' depends to a lesser extent on the plainchant. The style of the mass is more elaborate, and there are traces of the earlier manner—a theme being occasionally given to one part in long (breve) notes. This fact, coupled with the interpolated words in the 'Gloria,' 'Ad Mariae gloriam, Mariam coronans, Mariam gubernans,' etc., points to the six-part mass having been written earlier than the one in four parts. The latter may be regarded as an interesting experiment, also carried out in the masses entitled *In majoribus duplicibus* and *In minoribus duplicibus,* where the plainchant masses are utilized in a similar manner.

In the case of the two masses bearing the title of *Ave Maria* the more elaborate six-part work is also the earlier, on internal evidence, since a *canto fermo* in long notes with the words 'Ave Maria gratia plena' appears in every one of the movements. By writing at a later date a second mass, in simpler style, for four voices and with the same title Palestrina showed further signs of a desire to clarify his musical style. The four-part work is based upon the familiar melody—one of the most beautiful in Gregorian music—associated with the words of the Angelic Salutation:

This furnishes several *motifs*, all developed into a light, graceful musical texture in each movement. Special mention may be made of the 'Sanctus,' with its exquisite little 'Pleni sunt coeli' (for soprano, alto and tenor), a movement in most delicate decorative style, where, in some passages, only two voices are employed with charming effect.

Other masses in this group which deserve longer mention than can be accorded to them here are the *Regina coeli* and *Ave Regina coelorum* in four parts, the five-part *Salve Regina* and the six-part *Alma Redemptoris*, all founded upon the plain-chant antiphons for Compline. The first-named work has many beautiful moments, one in particular being the opening of the 'Sanctus,' where the first part of the antiphonal melody is given a charming undulating rhythm. In the *Salve Regina* the treatment of the familiar melody is equally happy.

A six-part mass that must be ranked with the *Assumpta est* —in the opinion of some it is even finer—is the great work written for the feast of All Saints, *Ecce ego Joannes*. Its title is derived from the words of the Apocalypse of St John: 'Ecce ego Joannes vidi alterum angelum ascendentem ab ortu solis . . .' The date of composition of this mass, the music of which, in Raugel's words, 'shines with an apocalyptic splendour,' is uncertain. It is usually assigned to the pontificate of Sixtus V (i.e. 1585-90), but a careful consideration of the music itself suggests that the period mentioned may only have been that during which it was completed or copied into the Papal Choir books (which provide the earliest extant manuscript). Haberl has pointed out that the six voices for which it is laid out—soprano, alto, two tenors, two basses—are the same as in the *Papae Marcelli*, to which work he considers *Ecce ego Joannes* superior. But the resemblance goes much farther than this: no one who has heard the two masses could fail to be impressed by other similarities; here is the same remote, mystic atmosphere, the same almost austere dignity in each, and when the musical structures of the two masses are compared further resemblances will be noticed. The *Ecce ego Joannes* has, like the *Papae Marcelli*, a short, simple theme of bold outline upon which much of the contrapuntal edifice rests, as upon a pedestal, and there is the same sober, restrained movement of the polyphony in each case. One may not be wrong, therefore, in thinking that the mass was actually written, or at any rate, begun soon after the *Papae Marcelli* was completed.

It is impossible, as in the case of the latter mass, to assign any very precise origin to the themes. Such scraps as are shown in this excerpt may derive from plainchant or other sources; or they may be original. In any case they are unimportant compared with the magnificent musical edifice produced by their aid:

The first is the most important and, as already mentioned, it is often used merely to support the musical fabric; but at times it strides majestically up and down, from voice to voice. A mystic touch is given to the music by the insistence on the flattened seventh of the Mixolydian mode in which the mass is written. It is shown in the excerpt given above, and is used with particularly beautiful effect in the melody which each voice takes up in turn in the 'Benedictus.' The 'Sanctus,' where all six voices are continually employed, is one of the finest parts of the mass, but the 'Gloria' and 'Credo,' magnificent in design, have also many superb passages.

The mass *Te Deum laudamus*, founded upon the melodies of the plainchant setting of the hymn, is one of those works to be admired more as superb examples of the composer's skill than for their purely musical qualities. The music, comparable in style to the *Papae Marcelli* and the *Ecce ego Joannes*, has a simple grandeur of design and an austerely solemn mood in keeping with the antique Phrygian mode plainchant.

An interesting feature of the mass is that in the 'Gloria' and 'Credo' Palestrina has altered the ascending minor third of the liturgical intonation to a major interval, using this in a way that suggests both the modern major and minor modes.

This brief and necessarily inadequate survey of the masses may be closed with some mention of three fine eight-part masses: the Christmas *Hodie Christus natus est,* the festal *Laudate Dominum* and *Fratres ego enim accepi.* All these are thematically connected with Palestrina's motets bearing the same titles, but whether the motets or the masses were composed first is not known. As far as the former are concerned, *Hodie Christus natus est* was published in 1575, *Laudate Dominum* appeared in 1572, while *Fratres ego enim accepi* was not published in Palestrina's lifetime. The date of publication of all three masses is 1601. At first sight, therefore, the two former would appear to have been composed after the motets, but one cannot be at all certain. Possibly Palestrina worked at the dual form more or less simultaneously and kept back the masses for further revision (which they may not have had, since he did not publish them in his lifetime). A comparison of the music in each case supports this view.

The Mass *Hodie Christus* has a charming naïvety of style, quite in keeping with the day it commemorates. The voices are grouped in two four-part choirs continually answering one another antiphonally in music that is always tinged with a feeling of rejoicing. The themes upon which it is constructed are quite simple and often give rise to carol-like passages.

The principal theme of the *Laudate Dominum* has already been quoted in a previous chapter (see page 85). Its elaborate contours set the style for most of the music, initiating a brilliant polyphony appropriate to the theme of praise suggested by the title. This and the other themes are apparently original, although the first two, announced in the 'Kyrie' and the 'Christe,' are possibly suggested by a Gregorian tone to which the psalm of the same title is sung, the outline of this being vaguely discernible in the music. In this mass also the anti-phonal effect between the choirs is so constant that it almost suggests a friendly competition between the two. Sometimes they echo each other; at other times a fine phrase from the first evokes an even finer one from the second; occasionally they join forces for special effects of sonority. The 'Credo' has a rather unusual feature: the eight voices are regrouped in the central part of the movement, choir No. 1 (two altos, tenor and bass) singing the 'Crucifixus,' No. 2 (two sopranos, tenor and bass) taking its turn at 'Et in Spiritum Sanctum.' The two are merged together for the finale.

The mass *Fratres ego enim accepi* is an interesting example of decorative polyphony applied to a large-scale design: although the music is laid out for the customary two groups each of four voices, these are more often combined than used separately. There is less homophony than usual in the 'Gloria' and 'Credo,' and the whole work gives one the impression of music in subdued but rich texture. As the words of the motet describe the institution of the Eucharist, it is possible that the mass was designed to be sung at Eucharistic festivals.

CHAPTER X

In musical value, as well as in number, Palestrina's motets form a part of his creative work next in importance to the masses. Mirrored in their music is, as it were, the whole life of the church—her days of gladness and rejoicing, and of sorrow, her seasons of penitence, her commemorations, her devotions, in short, all the manifold activities of the ecclesiastical year. As one would expect, therefore, the motets range over an immense field as regards variety of sentiment and style, form and design, since there is hardly a liturgical occasion for which Palestrina did not provide some music. And in many cases he has linked his own work closely to the liturgy by utilizing, as in the masses, the plainchant melodies as a source of thematic ideas, even in some instances weaving these melodies, with hardly any alteration, into his musical fabric. The motets number, if we include works in the same form— such as the offertories, psalm settings, hymns, etc.—between 400 and 500 pieces, varying from modest little movements in three or four parts, intended for everyday use, to magnificent and elaborate works (employing six, seven, eight and occasionally twelve parts) destined for great festivals and special occasions.

They show a greater variation in musical quality than the masses, which is perhaps not surprising in view of their number, although probably no other composer could have maintained such a high level of invention and workmanship as we find here, in this vast mass of music.

The finest of the motets rank with the masterpieces among

the masses in inspiration and workmanship, but, on the other hand, a certain proportion must be considered inferior to the rest. For this we should not altogether blame Palestrina, but rather the uninspiring nature, from a musical point of view, of some of the texts set, which are for the most part taken from the 'Proper' for feasts, commemorations and the ordinary times.[1]

The words of the 'Proper' are chosen not only from Holy Scripture, but from the religious poetry and prose of medieval times, and their infinite variety naturally offers a composer greater musical freedom than in the case of the mass, with its invariable text and the necessity for working more strictly within liturgical limits. Palestrina indeed found here an almost illimitable field for his genius, and the number of acknowledged masterpieces he produced therein is a sufficiently large proportion of the whole to be considered remarkable.

The existence of two, and sometimes even more, settings of the same text may be noted. Thus there are no fewer than five versions of the 'Salve Regina' (for four, five, six, eight and twelve voices respectively), four of the 'Ave Maria' (two four-part works, one in five and one in six parts) and a number of instances where three versions are to be found. Two fairly obvious reasons may be given for this: the first a liturgical one, the provision of a setting suitable for ordinary use, and another for special occasions; the second one that would naturally arise in the career of a church musician—a work written in earlier days for a choir of moderate attainments, and another in later years when better singers were available. The music of these duplications illustrates both.

Any attempt to classify the motets by assigning their composi-

---

[1] The meaning of the 'Proper' in relation to the mass has already been explained; the other services and the various offices of the church also have a part of their liturgy which varies according to the day or season of the year.

tion to various periods is even more difficult than in the case of the masses, for dates of publication are equally misleading and comparisons of style less easy owing to the varied nature of the motets.

Palestrina published a first collection of motets about 1563,[1] that is to say, when he was about thirty-seven, in the early maturity of his creative power. Other collections were issued by him in 1569, 1572, 1575, 1581, 1584 and 1593 (offertories). A large number remained in manuscript, distributed among the choir-books of the papal chapel, the Roman basilicas and other churches in the city, and most of these did not see the light until they found their way into nineteenth-century collections of Palestrina's works.

Some writers have attempted to draw an analogy between the masses and the motets on the one hand, and 'absolute' and 'programme' music on the other, but such an idea is apt to be misleading. The decorative principle is still the basis of Palestrina's musical style in his motets, although a new element of expression, which may be pictorial or descriptive, often governs the type of *motif* employed and its expansion.

In setting the particular text each phrase or idea of the words (sometimes a whole sentence, sometimes only one or two words) inspires in turn a corresponding musical idea, this being taken up by each voice to the same words and developed according to the musical and textual importance: a cadence or half-cadence leads to the exposition and treatment of the next textual-thematic *motif*, and so on. All this is in accordance with the principle previously enunciated—that the object of the music is to concentrate the attention of the listener upon the text and its significance.

An excellent illustration of this plan in actual working is

[1] No copy of the original edition is known to exist. A second edition, issued in 1571, survives in a single copy, and evidence connected with this suggests the date mentioned.

the familiar *Super flumina Babylonis*, where the first long, wailing phrase for the words just mentioned presents a picture of the lamenting exiles; a series of cadences, upon the words 'illic sedimus et flevimus,' brings us to the next section, built up on the infinitely poignant theme (taken from the plainchant setting) to which the next phrase, 'dum recordaremur tui Sion,' is developed. A further musical idea (allied to the first) takes up the words 'suspendemus organa nostra,' leading to the final part of the motet.

The motets of the 1563 book, which are all in four parts, seem to be for the most part early works, some of them possibly written during Palestrina's service at St Agapit's, i.e. between 1544 and 1551. Only a few of the thirty-six contained in this first collection are of any striking quality: when they are compared to the four-part motets issued in 1581, among which are masterpieces such as the motet just mentioned and *Sicut cervus*, the difference is at once apparent.

They are for the most part short, the texts being generally taken from the antiphons of the Vesperale for feasts and the commemoration of saints ('Commune Sanctorum'), while a large proportion of them are thematically dependent upon the plainchant associated with the words. The melody is either used with slight modification or its contours provide an element from which themes are developed.

Whatever their precise musical value, we can see, in these early pieces, how Palestrina had already begun to form a style of design which was to develop so wonderfully in the later great works in motet form. We find here the beginnings of that simplicity and dignity which, at an early stage, differentiated his music from that of most of his immediate predecessors and contemporaries in the polyphonic field. There is already a grace and a suavity (and sometimes a restraint) in the polyphony; the latter alternates with homophonic passages of simple yet beautiful effect; the variety of metre and rhythmic freedom are already beginning to be noticeable.

The best of these earlier works are the charming little Nativity motet, *Dies sanctificatus*; the exquisite *Salvator mundi*; *Valde honorandus est* (for the feast of St John the Evangelist); *O quantus luctus* (commemorating St Martin); and *Veni sponsa Christi* (for a virgin martyr).

There is an attractive charm about the simple naïvety of the first-named work: it is mainly homophonic, and much of the music has almost the effect of a carol, especially the last part, which begins with this beautiful strain:

The second (*Salvator mundi*) might almost be described as a sung prayer: it commences with a quiet devotional setting of the first sentence, 'Salvator mundi, salva nos omnes,' this being followed by various invocations for the intercession of Our Lady, the Saints, Patriarchs, Martyrs, etc., all of which are set to tender, appealing, litany-like music.

Veni sponsa Christi is delicately woven in a graceful poly-phonic design, out of the simple, almost wistful plainchant melody in the Vesperale, this being divided into two or three *motifs*. Out of the first is developed, and thrice repeated with slight variation, the setting of the salutation which forms the title of the motet. The words 'accipe coronam' are similarly treated, with the theme at a higher pitch on each repetition; in the third and final musical stanza of this brief but beautiful piece the words 'quam tibi Dominum praeparavit' are set to the plainchant *motif* for this phrase just as it stands, with each voice taking it up in turn.

The music of *Valde honorandus est*, based upon the Gregorian antiphon, is carried out in tender, suave lines, appropriate to a picture of the 'loved disciple' commemorated in the words. *O quantus luctus* derives its effect mainly from the bold theme, opening with an upward leap of an octave, which is constantly in evidence through the contrapuntal fabric. By some writers the early *Ave Maria* is included among the best of these 1563 motets, but it is not to be compared with Palestrina's later settings of the Angelic Salutation: there is, for example, a finer four-part work in the 1581 book.

Possibly a few of the motets which are to be found in the latter may have been in existence at the time when the earlier collection was issued, but eighteen years later some magnificent works in the same form were added to them, composed during the 1570's, when Palestrina's creative gift seems to have functioned inexhaustibly.

The 1581 book contains twenty-one motets (some of which are in two separate parts) with texts taken from responses, psalms and antiphons. Ten of them are written for the usual four-part combination (soprano, alto, tenor and bass), but in the others we find Palestrina continuing those experiments in vocal tone-colour which were to be noticed in the masses. Five are set for three soprano parts and alto; three for two soprano parts, alto and tenor; two for alto, two tenor parts and bass; and one for three soprano parts and tenor.

Among the best are the *Super flumina Babylonis* already mentioned; others almost ranking with it are the beautiful *Sicut cervus* (sung at the blessing of the baptismal font on Holy Saturday), *Ad te levavi* (Compline psalm for All Souls' Day), *Adoramus te Christe*, *Pueri Hebraeorum* (sung on Palm Sunday) and a group of settings of the antiphons of the Blessed Virgin—*Ave Maria*, *Ave Regina coelorum*, *Salve Regina* and *Alma Redemptoris*.

The first-named work is unquestionably one of the greatest pieces of music that ever came from Palestrina's pen. No composer in any age ever wrote anything with a greater power to evoke in the mind of the listener the anguished remembrance of vanished happiness than the passage shown on page 141, which, twice repeated, each time with more tensely drawn contrapuntal lines, forms the great central climax of the motet, and the second of the three divisions into which the music falls, following the opening part with its long lamenting phrases, and preceding the concluding picture inspired by the words 'in salicibus in medio ejus suspendimus organa nostra.'

Sicut cervus, in the opinion of many, ranks almost with the motet just discussed. Its music has a grace and freshness and a limpidity in its polyphony that seems to be suggested by the thirst-quenching springs of which the psalmist speaks. The principal theme, given to the tenor at the commencement of the motet, is graceful enough to deserve the description applied to it by Raugel: 'Fraîche comme une chanson de France.'

An exquisite miniature is *Adoramus te Christe*, which one might describe as a sung prayer; the polyphony hardly moves, except for tiny decorative touches at each mention of the Saviour, and is often merged into simple harmonies.

An admirable illustration of the pictorial and descriptive style Palestrina so frequently employs in these motets is furnished by *Pueri Hebraeorum,* one of the antiphons intended to be sung during the distribution of the palm branches on Palm Sunday. It is a vivid little tone-poem, painting the scene during Christ's entry into Jerusalem. The choice of voices—two sopranos, alto and tenor—is possibly meant to suggest a gathering of boys and youths of varying ages; the opening strains, with each part swiftly entering in turn, evidently pictures the little band assembling, and the succeeding simple, march-like passage their advance, 'portantes ramos,' to meet the Saviour. The polyphonic movement is resumed as the text describes their greeting to Him, and towards the end little decorative touches appear in the contrapuntal melodies, symbolizing the waving of the branches as the procession moves on into Jerusalem to the cries of 'Osanna.'

The pictorial element may again be observed in *Ad te levavi oculos*, where the principal theme (with its charming effect from the prominent flattened seventh of the modal scale):

continually soars up in illustration of the psalmist's words: 'To Thee have I lifted up mine eyes, Thou who dwellest in heaven.' This motet is particularly interesting because of its bright, animated, almost secular, character, recalling the style of a madrigal. Perhaps we may regard it as a foretaste of that 'genus alacrius' which three years later Palestrina tells us he had employed in setting the Song of Songs.

The music sustains its light, vivacious character until the final words with their appeal for mercy—'misereatur nostri donec'—bring a quiet ending to this most charming piece.

Among the group of antiphons of the Blessed Virgin the best is undoubtedly the *Ave Regina coelorum*, for three sopranos and alto, a piece of diaphanous tonal texture woven out of themes freely adapted from the plainchant setting of the antiphon. It begins with a graceful musical elaboration of the salutation ('Ave') to an undulating theme introduced by the alto and taken up in turn by each soprano part at the same pitch, producing a charming kind of echo effect. The 'Ave' is repeated after the words 'Regina coelorum' have been developed to another equally decorative *motif*, symbolical of the Blessed Virgin herself, and subsequently utilized for the next appellation 'Domina angelorum.'

For the motet in five-part form Palestrina seems to have had a special predilection: if we include the offertories, published in 1593, and written in this same style, nearly 200 such pieces saw the light between 1569 and the date just mentioned. As compared with four-part writing the extra voice allowed a slightly richer and fuller polyphony and also a more varied choice of vocal tone-colour, without making the music too elaborate, and in this connection it may be of interest to point out that for one of his greatest works—the setting of the Song of Songs—this particular form was chosen by the composer.

In such a vast collection as these five-part motets represent there must necessarily be a certain number showing signs of having been composed as a matter of routine rather than as the result of inspiration; but even the most critical survey of them must result in allowing the musical merit of a considerable proportion to be on a high level, and bestowing upon a certain number the distinction of masterpieces worthy to rank with the best of Palestrina's music in other directions.

One of the most remarkable of the latter is the penitential *Peccantem me quotidie*; here is music which again prompts the remark made in the previous chapter, that Palestrina's musical vision sometimes projected itself far into the future. Such a passage as this would hardly seem 'dated' even two centuries later:

This motet is a wonderful piece of work. The theme marked (*a*), with its rising fourth and falling semitones, is a picture of the sinner tormented by the fear of hell; its melancholy cadences haunt the first part of the movement, until a new musical idea, the spectre of Death ('Timor mortis conturbat me') almost seems to confront us in this phrase:

In the third part of the motet, devoted to a setting of the words 'miserere mei Deus, et salva me,' the music has an exquisitely pathetic appeal, as the quotation on page 147 shows. In this motet, indeed, one feels that Palestrina has more nearly approached the modern conception of emotional expression in music than in almost anything else he wrote.

No more striking illustration of the range to be found in his creative art could be afforded than by turning from the elegiac mood of *Peccantem me quotidie* to the festal *Exultate Deo*. In this splendid piece of joyful music we find ingenious semi-

realistic suggestions of instrumental effects, illustrating the psalmist's exhortation to praise the Lord: 'Sumite psalmum, et date tympanum, psalterium jucundum cum cithara, buccinate in neomenia tuba.' After a brilliant opening, built upon a theme of rejoicing, we have a quaintly charming little picture of this tiny 'orchestra.' The psalmum (according to Stainer's *Music of the Bible* a kind of pipes) does not seem to be associated with any particular *motif*, but the psalterium (a species of dulcimer), the drum, the cithara (or lyra) and the trumpet are easily identifiable in this excerpt:

147

from the middle part of the motet, which winds up with an appropriately dignified treatment of the concluding words, 'insigne die solemnitatis vestrae.'

But with this familiar pictorial-descriptive style which was his favourite method, Palestrina could produce equally impressive effects of another kind, even a dramatic intensity, as we may see in the Advent-tide *Canite tuba in Sion*, where the long-drawn-out opening suggests a solemn fanfare ('Sound the trumpet in Sion') which also brings with it a tense, expectant

feeling: the music grows more animated, suggesting the excite-
ment over 'Him who comes to save us,' then quiets down as
groups of three voices tell one another of 'the crooked paths
made straight' and 'the rough places made plain,' to surge up
suddenly in the realistic cry: 'Come, O Lord.'

The first part of the motet closes with serenely dignified
Alleluias, the second part ('Rorate coeli') opening with another
solemn quasi-trumpet *motif*: the cry 'Come, O Lord' is
reiterated with a more tensely woven polyphony, then the
Alleluias of the first part reappear for the finale.

Brief mention only can be made of a number of other fine
motets which would deserve detailed consideration in a
lengthier survey than is possible here. A paean of praise
which should be coupled with the *Exultate Deo* just described
is the motet entitled *Alleluia tulerunt Dominum*. In his treatment
of the Alleluia, here and in other motets, Palestrina, freed from
all textual restrictions, was able to give full play to his genius
for purely decorative writing: the lines sweep up and down with
a magnificent rhythmic surge, producing richly sonorous sound
patterns, these being repeated at intervals, interspersed with the
text, thus giving to the whole motet a remarkable brilliance of
effect: another attractive specimen of the Palestrinian Alleluia
is to be found in the motet *O beata et gloriosa Trinitas*.

A few lines must also be spared for two eucharistic motets,
Ego sum panis vivus (with its second part 'Panis quem ego dabo')
and *O sacrum convivium*, the former notable for the dignified
simplicity of the contrapuntal writing, the latter deriving much
of its charm from a skilful treatment of the beautiful plainchant
melody belonging to the antiphon. Mention should also be
made of another motet of praise—*Jubilate Deo*, a splendidly
sonorous setting of the 99th Psalm.

As in the case of the four-part motets, we also find among
those in five-part form a group of settings of the antiphons in

honour of the Blessed Virgin, the best of which are the *Salve Regina* and the *Ave Regina coelorum*. The music of the first-named is of the most delicate beauty. In its vocal writing the composer aimed at producing the most translucent tone possible, not only by the choice of voices (two sopranos, alto and two tenors) and the use of particular registers of those voices, but also by keeping the contrapuntal texture light and graceful.

The two sets of offertories in five parts, covering the whole of the ecclesiastical year, although not issued by Palestrina until 1593, a few months before his death, contain a certain number of pieces that were probably composed many years earlier, as their texts are not in conformity with the revised missal issued in 1570 by Pius V. But although written at various periods, these offertories were apparently planned out as a complete scheme, from the musical point of view, to present a tonal picture of the liturgical year, illustrating its high lights (the great festivals) as well as the deep shadows of Lent and Advent; accordingly the music of the motets shows a graduation from one point to another. The Advent motets, for example, begin with the sombre music of *Ad te Domine levavi* (not to be confused with the four-part work mentioned previously); then in the offertories for the succeeding Sundays there is a gradual lightening of style, until, with the Christmas *Tui sunt coeli*, their music becomes filled with joy and gladness. A similar progression is to be observed from the first Sunday of Lent until Easter Sunday. In the second set may be found one of the very finest of the whole sixty-eight offertories, the Ash Wednesday *Exaltabo te Domine*.[1] This is indeed to be ranked among the greatest of the motets, and the enthusiasm expressed for its music by Baini and other writers is pardonable, because of its sustained elevation and nobility of style, matching the deep sincerity of thanksgiving expressed in the psalmist's

[1] It is also the offertory for the eleventh Sunday after Pentecost.

words: 'I will extol Thee, O Lord, for Thou hast lifted
me up and hast not made my foes to triumph over me.'
The music follows out the now familiar Palestrinian plan of
taking in turn each phrase or idea of the text for illustration.
And so in the opening a serenely dignified theme is developed
in spacious polyphony, to the words 'Exaltabo te, Domine.'
The passage which follows, upon 'quoniam suscepisti me,' is
almost unsurpassed for beauty by any other of Palestrina's
motets, as this quotation will show:

The expressive theme which forms its basis, first enunciated by the bass, gradually rises with fine effect through the voices, terminating with a beautiful decorative figure in the soprano. Equally striking is this superb polyphonic phrase upon the words 'nec delectasti,' probably meant as an expression of delight at escaping from the enemy (*see below*).

Its beautiful cadence at the words 'inimicos meos super me' is repeated, and after a simple but bold treatment of the prayer 'Domine, clamavi ad te,' the motet concludes with a tranquil passage, where a descending figure pictures the healing 'et sanasti me.'

Compared with those in four and five parts, Palestrina's six-part motets are few in number. During his lifetime thirty

[musical notation]

of them were issued, among the collections of motets issued in
1569, 1572 and 1575. The complete edition of Breitkopf &
Härtel prints a dozen more, collected from the choir-books of
the papal singers and other sources. Probably most of these
motets, the general level of which, musically, is perhaps below
that of the five-part works, were composed after Palestrina had
settled down in Rome; at least half a dozen of them are of
outstanding quality, meriting brief description. One of them
seems, in fact, to have been particularly highly esteemed by the
composer himself—the motet entitled *Accepit Jesus calicem*, for, according to Raugel, in one of the Vatican portraits of Palestrina the
artist depicted him with the manuscript of this work in one hand.
It is certainly music of great beauty, and interesting technically
because of its canonic form—'three in one,' with double resolution at the fourth and the octave—the composer's intention being
to make, in the music, a mystical allusion to the Trinity.

An original touch is to be found in the six-part penitential
motet, *Tribularer si nescirem*, where the alto constantly intones this
supplication:

in the midst of the sombre polyphony; at each repetition the voice rises a tone higher until it reaches a fifth above, then descends by similar repetitions.

But an even more beautiful specimen of Palestrina's six-part writing is the pentecostal *Dum complerentur* (belonging to the 1569 motet book and probably composed only shortly before that date), a work remarkable alike for breadth of design and beauty of idea. The suggestiveness of his pictorial style is again admirably illustrated in the opening moments, where the stillness of dawn, as the little band of Apostles and the faithful wait in hushed expectancy in that upper room, seems perfectly reflected in those tranquil sustained chords (first in three parts, then four and finally six), with only an occasional contrapuntal ripple disturbing their serenity:

Here, as in so many other instances, one feels that the composer's conception is almost instrumental in style, for the passage quoted—to which the opening words describing the scene on that first Pentecost day are set—would be equally effective if played, for example, by stringed instruments, making indeed an ideal prelude to the exquisite Alleluia that follows, a greeting to the eagerly awaited Holy Spirit. The narration proceeds; the voices echo 'et subito' after each other: the 'sonus de coelo' is depicted by a downward-rushing figure, another Alleluia breaking in upon this. The coming of the 'spiritus vehemens' ('the mighty wind') is quietly announced, but a polyphonic movement begins and expands, to the words 'et replevit totam domum,' describing how 'the whole house was filled.' The central climax of the motet is now reached—an elaborate Alleluia of joy and praise and thanksgiving, in which there is a suggestion of the heavenly host joining in with the worshippers on earth. The first tenor leads off with the long, decorative *motif*, the rest of the voices gradually entering until at length the whole six parts weave a brilliant fabric of sound, bringing the first part of the motet to a conclusion. The second part, *Dum ergo essent*, follows to some extent the plan of the first: gently moving phrases suggest the assembling of the faithful 'in fear of the Jews'; and again the 'sudden sound from heaven' is announced, this time to a theme that swiftly descends a whole octave, passed from one group of voices to another, and broadening out into a stately movement at the words 'venit super eos.' The remainder is mostly a repeat of the first part, winding up with the great Alleluia previously heard.

Some beautiful and original features distinguish the music of the Christmastide *O magnum mysterium*. These first three words of the text are set to music of delightful naïvety, an expression of almost childlike wonder at the mystery of the Incarnation:

It is a pretty little picture of astonishment: the first and second sopranos, first alto and first tenor sing 'O,' long drawn out, to three sustained chords; the second tenor and bass, after a preliminary ejaculation, are silent for a few moments, in seeming bewilderment, and do not join the rest in the fine, broad phrase emphasiing the word 'mysterium.' All voices then repeat 'O magnum mysterium,' but in a calmer manner, for the first feeling of astonishment has subsided. There is still a sense of mystery and awe, however, in the quiet music which follows, with its restrained touches of polyphony, describing how 'animalia viderunt Dominum natum in praesepio.' A simple Alleluia concludes the first part of the motet.

The music of the second part ('Quem vidistis, pastores?') begins with a charming pastoral touch, bringing before the listener the familiar story of the 'shepherds abiding in the fields.' Two little duets following one another have themes of rustic flavour, almost a suggestion of pipe tunes; with this is presently contrasted some music of simple dignity, an echo of the 'choros angelorum collaudantes Dominum,' the motet concluding with the Alleluia belonging to the first part.

A companion work to the Mass *Assumpta est Maria*, the six-part motet of the same name, written also for the feast of the Assumption, has for a principal theme the same subject which is so much used in the mass (taken from the plainchant setting of the antiphon). The music, however, is not in any way a repetition of the latter, although the two works have some characteristics in common, especially in the brilliant decorative style of the music, woven in florid figures symbolical of the festal rejoicing in which, to quote the text of the antiphon, 'the angels join.'

The principal theme is developed in the opening part of the motet and culminates in a climax, after which a second strain, for the exhortation 'gaudete et exultate,' is introduced, forming the basis of another richly woven contrapuntal passage. The second part, 'Quae est ista,' [1] begins quietly, in a mystic mood appropriate to the symbolical text, but the note of rejoicing soon returns, and the earlier music, with its elaborate polyphony, is repeated.

Considered by many to rank with the best of these six-part works is the Ascension-tide *Viri Galilaei*: the elegiac quality of its music expresses the desolation of the 'men of Galilee' and brings vividly to the mind the picture of them, gazing heaven-ward as their beloved Master is lost to sight; even the Alleluia at the end is tinged with melancholy. The second part, pic-turing the actual Ascension, opens with the development of a *motif* ascending a complete octave, a tiny fanfare-like figure being added for the 'voce tubae.' The music here is of joyful character, but at the end the reappearance of the Alleluia of the earlier part brings once more a tinge of sadness.

The Easter *Haec dies*, with its lovely Alleluia; the apocalyptic *Vidi turbam magnam*; *O bone Jesu*, of devotional beauty, and *Tradent enim vos* (vespers antiphon for the commemoration of

---

[1] The text here is taken from the Song of Solomon, and is symboli-cally applied to the Blessed Virgin; it has also been utilized by Palestrina in his setting of that work.

Apostles and Evangelists) are also notable examples of Palestrina's six-part writing, though they can only be given bare mention here.

There are two seven-part works to be found among the motets. Of these only the first need be cited: the setting of *Tu es Petrus* (belonging to the feast of SS. Peter and Paul), usually sung at solemn functions whenever the pope (as successor to St Peter) is present. The music of this motet, broad and dignified in style, is developed on *motifs* adapted from the plainchant setting of the antiphon. The bold upward leap of an octave in the figure associated with the church ('super hanc petram aedificabo ecclesiam') makes a striking effect in the latter part of this short but impressive piece.

More than fifty motets in eight parts are included in the collected edition of Palestrina's works, but of these only ten were printed during his lifetime—in the motet books which appeared in 1572 and 1575. Many of the others, of course, were known and sung in the composer's day, existing at his death only in manuscript, some in the Papal Choir books, others in various Roman churches.

In these motets, as in the greater masses, the musical design takes an architectural form: most of them are planned for two choirs, each of four parts, but from time to time they are combined to build up big masses of tone. In some of these works the continued antiphonal effect of the two choirs, often merely repeating the same passage, tends to a monotony of effect. Elsewhere, on the other hand, the composer uses the whole eight voices with wonderful skill, combining them in great variety and thereby obtaining a fine range of musical effect.

The greatest of all the eight-part works is *Surge illuminare*, which from the time of its composition (about 1574) to the present day has been sung every year at Epiphany in the Sistine Chapel. It employs the voices mostly in the two groups, but with such superb skill and sense of effect that the motet is rightly regarded as one of the noblest pieces of music Palestrina wrote. Many commentators have justly praised it for the magnificent breadth and sweep of its design, which Baini compares to a work by Michelangelo. The mystical radiance of which the prophetic words speak seems reflected in the opening of the motet—a majestic outburst of polyphony from the first choir on the word 'surge' (which is repeated), the voices soaring up and slowing down for a cadence at the word 'Hierusalem':

The second choir answers quietly, and a moment or two later the two join forces in a stupendous passage, at the words 'et gloria Domini super te orta est,' where the majestic rhythm and the massive progressions—a succession of major triads in Palestrina's characteristic manner—give the homophony a definitely harmonic character. With a fine sense of contrast the first choir follows this in quiet expressive harmonies ('quia ecce tenebrae operient terram'), this mood continuing until the prophecy 'orietur Dominus et gloria ejus in te videbitur' initiates once more a polyphonic movement in the same fine, broad sweep that characterized the opening, and now leading to an impressive conclusion where the two choirs seem to vie with each other in stately phrases proclaiming 'gloria ejus.' The so-called second part of the motet, 'Et ambulabant gentes in lumine tuo,' hardly belongs to it artistically, since its music was written some years after the first part. By comparison it is certainly inferior, although by no means so poor as some critics aver.

A similarity of style between the music of *Surge illuminare* and the eight-part *Jubilate Deo*, composed for the opening of the Holy Door at Christmas 1574 (inaugurating the jubilee year 1575), may be explained by the fact that both seem to have been written about the same period. There is the same splendidly vigorous movement at the outset, a bold sweep of the contrapuntal lines rising up in a similar way to a broad climax—a perfect musical counterpart to the joyous mood of the psalmist. In this fine introduction and for most of the remainder of the motet the two choirs generally answer each other, the music varying between passages of harmonic effect and a dignified polyphony. Occasionally all the eight voices are combined to give emphasis to particular ideas: for example at the words 'populus' and 'in confessione' in the sentence 'populus ejus et oves pascuae ejus, introite portas ejus in confessione.' The motet concludes with a fine 'Gloria' in triple-time rhythm.

A piece of writing showing the eight parts (although nominally grouped into the two choirs) more intermingled is the setting of another psalm, *Laudate pueri Dominum* (Ps. 112). The voices enter one by one at the beginning and are constantly continued in various ways for different effects suggested by the words: the close imitative weaving of the parts gives a particular firmness and strength to the tonal texture, as well as adding to the effect of the music, with its spacious lines.

Another masterpiece among the eight-part works is the Nativity motet *Hodie Christus natus est*. Here again we find a charmingly naïve touch: the composer has endeavoured to visualize for us the rejoicing of the people at the birth of the Saviour, a glimpse of the Christmas scene in medieval times, when even the people in the streets cried aloud the glad tidings to each other.[1] And so, repeated throughout this motet, we hear their joyful shouts of 'Noel, Noel' interrupting the narrative, and, from a musical point of view, providing novel and beautiful cadences to the various sentences of the antiphon text. The two choirs continually answer each other with this Christmas greeting. Beginning quietly, the music grows in splendour and brilliance at the mention of the heavenly rejoicing ('canunt angeli, laetantur archangeli'), until a great climax is reached where the two choirs combine in a majestic 'gloria in excelsis.' The strains of this die away—picturing the fading of the heavenly vision—and we are left with the rejoicings on earth, the motet closing with repeated 'Noels.'

The usual group of settings of the antiphons of the Blessed Virgin is to be found also among the eight-part motets, the *Ave Maria*, *Salve Regina*, *Ave Regina coelorum*, *Alma Redemptoris* and *Regina coeli*. The second of these must be singled out for brief description. Its music is remarkable for the sombre mood, sustained almost throughout the movement, emphasizing the picture presented in the text: 'To Thee do we cry, poor banished children of Eve, to Thee do we send up our sighs, mourning and weeping in this vale of tears.'[2] Its dramatic

[1] The custom still survives in Russia.

[2] The words are taken from the familiar English version of the antiphon.

qualities are no less notable: the bold declamatory music at the words 'ad te clamamus, exules Hevae,' the almost wailing phrases, 'gementes et flentes' and 'in lacrimarum valle,' the sudden loveliness of the music at the words 'et Jesum,' the graceful decorative treatment of the final apostrophe, 'O clemens, o pia, o dulcis Virgo Maria,' with each adjective repeated from choir to choir.

The eight-part settings of the great sequences—the *Lauda Sion* (from the mass of Corpus Christi), the *Veni Sancte spiritus* (sung at Pentecost) and *Haec dies* (from the Easter mass) are in motet form. Of all three there are two separate versions, in each case for double choir, one being apparently an earlier work, the other written some years later. Only one of each of the two first-named was published in Palestrina's lifetime, printed in the 1575 motet book, these being, no doubt, the later compositions, preferred by the composer himself.

As far as the *Veni Sancte Spiritus* is concerned the other setting is to be found in the library of the Roman Seminary, where Palestrina was musical director from 1565 to 1570, and in all probability it was written during that period. The continued employment of a triple-time rhythm in this earlier work, the somewhat rigid alternation of the two choirs and the note-against-note treatment, for the most part, of the plainchant melody, all contrast unfavourably with the other, where the rhythms are more elastic and varied, the melody treated with greater freedom and with more contrapuntal ornamentation.

The same comparison can be made between the two *Lauda Sion* versions, one of which sets the whole text of this somewhat lengthy sequence, the other only the opening and concluding portions, to which a certain amount of elaboration is given, the middle part being apparently intended to be sung to the original plainchant.

The book of *Hymni totius anni*, issued by the composer in

1589, presents an interesting study in the treatment of plain-chant. There are forty-five of them, mostly the vesper hymns, and in every case their music is founded on the beautiful old tunes associated with the words. The form is generally that of a species of choral variation. In some, the familiar *Veni Creator* for instance, the plainchant melody is treated quite simply; in others there is more elaboration, and the melody is developed with greater freedom, while the contrapuntal struc-ture is built up generally from the theme itself. In the longer hymns only a certain number of verses are set, these being intended, in performance, to alternate with the others sung to the plainchant version, a simple plan producing a fine effect, as those who have heard the processional *Vexilla Regis* and *Pange lingua* know. In the former the entry of the four voices at the words 'O Crux ave, spes unica' is wonderfully impres-sive following the simple plainchant verse. Another interesting point in these hymns is the variation in the number of parts employed, different verses being in some cases set for three, four or five and six voices.

The so-called twelve-part motets, printed in the complete (Breitkopf & Härtel) edition, consist of four psalms, a *Salve Regina* and a motet, *O quam bonus*. They are set for triple choir, each of four parts, but the third choir parts are apparently mostly missing in the contemporary manuscript copies of these works, since what is printed in the edition mentioned is described as having been supplied by Fr Michael Haller, the well-known Palestrinian scholar. In the *Salve Regina* the three choirs are merely employed in a short concluding section, the rest being in four and eight parts only, and neither this nor the other five works can be considered as representing the composer at his best.

CHAPTER XI

MADRIGALS, SECULAR AND SPIRITUAL

As a young man Palestrina seems to have cultivated madrigal writing assiduously, judging by the fact that before a note of any masses or motets from his pen had appeared in print, he had won sufficient recognition in this secular field for a madrigal, *Con dolce, altiero*, to be included in a collection by various composers issued at Venice early in 1554.

In the composer's youthful days the madrigal was still something of a novelty, and in common with other young musicians of his generation he was, no doubt, attracted by this new type of secular vocal music that was rapidly ousting the older forms —the *frottole*, the *stornelli* and the *strambotti*—from popular favour. The madrigal was also a possible source of financial gain, as apparently commissions were sometimes to be obtained from publishers issuing collections in different styles and eager to order new pieces from any composer who had begun to make a name for himself.

However, that sound judgment which characterized Palestrina, both as man and musician, must have made him realize, at an early stage in his career, that the secular madrigal offered no real opportunity for his particular creative gift. The sentiment of the type of poem that had to be set, especially the love-lyric, was apparently quite foreign to his essentially sober and serious turn of mind, which was incapable of translating anything like passion into music. Nevertheless the criticisms which have been directed against Palestrina's madrigals, for their motet-like style, their semi-religious atmosphere, are often too severe. An extreme case is that of Berlioz's remarks about 'madrigals in which the most frivolous and gallant words are set to exactly the same music as those of the Bible . . . the truth is that he could not write any other kind of music.'[1]

There is just a grain of truth in this: some of the madrigals, especially the earlier ones, are undoubtedly rather heavy in style, and it may be pointed out that Palestrina himself has admitted the partial truth of this criticism, as far as two madrigals are concerned, by taking the themes of these to serve as a basis for masses, *Vestiva i colli* and *Già fu chi m' ebbe cara.* Their themes needed, indeed, but very little adaptation to make them look liturgical, as, for example, these subjects from the last-named two madrigals, which suggest the dignified 'Kyries' they become in the masses:

---

[1] The quotation is from Mr Ernest Newman's admirable translation of Berlioz's *Memoirs.*

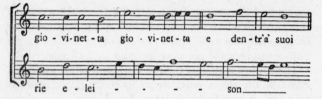

gio - vi - net - ta   gio - vi - net - ta   e   den - tr'a' suoi

rie   e - lei - - - - son_____

Both the madrigals just mentioned are probably quite early compositions: the somewhat austere and angular lines of *Vestiva i colli* are not particularly appropriate to the springtide picture described by the poem, and *Già fu chi m' ebbe cara* is only saved from a motet-like atmosphere and given a semblance of the romance underlying the words by imparting a rhythmic lilt to its staid melodies. Nevertheless such a creative gift of the first order as Palestrina's could not fail to enrich any musical form to which he might turn his attention, and a number of really fine pieces of music are to be found among the madrigals, particularly those where the words express the more lofty sentiments or portray pastoral scenes or extol the beauties of nature. Some of them, too, possess a special interest for the student, on account of the signs of experiment in chromatic and dissonant harmony they bear.

Palestrina's purely secular madrigals number about 100 pieces, varying from three-part movements to works in eight parts. The great bulk of them was probably composed before about 1565, only a few apparently belonging to any later period, and they were mostly written for special occasions, some perhaps while he was in the service of Cardinal d' Este, when the latter would entertain some personage of high rank with a musical performance at the magnificent Tivoli villa; others for various events—the victory over the Turks at Lepanto in 1571, for the rejoicings over which he composed the well-known *Le selv' avea*, the death of his friend the poet Annibale

Caro in 1566, one or two wedding festivities of the Roman aristocracy, and so on. It is quite certain that he had ceased to compose madrigals regularly some years before his public disavowal of such music in 1584.[1]

Palestrina himself issued two books of secular madrigals, and a considerable number also appeared in the many collections issued from time to time at Rome, Venice and other Italian cities by different publishers. Of the two books mentioned, the first is thought to have been printed in 1555, but no trace of this original edition survives: a volume appearing in 1568 and described as 'nuovamente ristampata' is considered to be a reprint of the earlier volume. The second collection dates from 1586.

Viewed as a whole the madrigals show a great diversity in musical style. Some of them certainly have something of the character of a motet; others have a rather squarecut homophonic form not always in keeping with the words. The best, however, possess a certain quality, a grace and charm, that distinguishes them quite definitely from the church music. The decorative style here has an appropriate lightness of touch and the pictorialdescriptive method is applied with the happiest results. Palestrina shows, indeed, that he could even be a miniaturist, as in the two tiny threepart canzonettas (for soprano, alto and tenor) which show an exquisite delicacy of manner, especially the plaintive *Ahi, che quest' occhi miei*.

The best of the fourpart madrigals are to be found in the 1586 book, in which are a number that have been justly admired. *Alla riva del Tebro* has a pastorallike opening, presently giving place to pungent discords, expressing the grief of the shepherd wandering by Tiber's banks, whose lamenting cry 'Ahi, miserabile sorte' is echoed from voice to voice as a

---

[1] See Chapter I, pp. 4, 5.

climax to a piece one might almost describe as a miniature tone-poem.

I vaghi fiori has a formal prettiness, its music patterned mostly from this one theme, which seems to typify the beauty of nature described by the poet—the lovely flowers, the foliage, the breeze, the cool shade:

With one dexterous touch, merely a slight rhythmic alteration, the melody becomes at the end tinged with sadness for the unfortunate being who can find no joy in all this beauty.

In quite a different vein is *Donna gentil*, a musical portrait where, in quiet, graceful melodic lines, the composer delineates the 'sweet lady, like the sun among the lesser stars,' whose face the poet longs to see and in whose presence strife and arrogance vanish. A tiny figure with which this madrigal opens seems to act as a *motif* representative of the 'donna gentil,' recurring in various guises from time to time.

The dainty freshness of *Amor, ben puoi*; the melodic beauty of *Morì quasi il mio core*; *O che splendor de' luminosi rai*, with its superb theme, building up an impression of light and splendour in keeping with the mystic poem; the remarkable dissonances with which *La cruda mia nemica* begins; the quiet impressive harmonies of *Vaghi pensier*; the stately beauty of *Quai rime,* in which poet and composer apostrophize Roussel [1] ('What rhymes, however bright, however lauded, could be worthy of thy music, Roussel,') single these madrigals out from the rest.

Among the five,part madrigals there is one work of out, standing originality and beauty: *Soave fia il morir*. The subject of the text, the sure hope of life after death, is of a kind one would naturally have expected to appeal to a composer so deeply religious as Palestrina, and it did in fact inspire him to write music of rare imaginative quality, interesting not only for its poetic, mystic atmosphere, but for its technical cleverness, its suggestion of changing tonalities, its 'orchestral' writing for the voices, its extraordinarily vivid descriptive power. Begin, ning with soft sustained chords to the opening words, 'Soave fia il morir,' the voices presently descend to their lowest registers as they sing of the 'closed eyes,' then spring up with a tiny figure that moves with an inexpressible lightness, picturing them 'opened for ever'; this leads to a remarkable passage, a few bars from which must be quoted, where the music, describing the 'clear bright abode,' expands out into a passage of almost Wagnerian grandeur (*see* p. 170).

Here the little fanfare,like figure, repeated from voice to voice, may possibly be a suggestion of the apocalyptic trumpet, call. The close of the madrigal, where soprano and tenor sustain a low note, while altos and basses softly chant of 'that bright adventurous day,' is a final effect worthy of the rest.

[1] Francesco Roussel, one of Palestrina's predecessors at Santa Maria Maggiore.

Another five-part madrigal which may be singled out is the lament for Endymion, *Il dolce sonno*, where the somnolent theme and the gentle, undulating movement of the voices combine to create a vague nebulous atmosphere in keeping with the poetic idea of 'sweet slumber, wherein Endymion lies entombed.' For a moment the music quickens into life at the words 'per baciar mille volte il tuo bel viso' ('to kiss thy fair face a thousand times'), then subsides again into its former dreaming mood, at the picture of the sleeping Endymion—'Io pur ti bacio, e tocco e tu non senti' ('I may kiss thee, touch thee, and thou knowest not').

Other fine examples of Palestrina's five-part madrigals are the plaintively melodious *Io son ferito*; the spirited and graceful *O bella Ninfa mia*; *Placide l' acque*, in which may be found one or two naïve examples of word painting—quiet chords for the 'still waters,' rapid moving figures for the wind and the waves. *Dido, chi giace* deserves special notice because of a curious feature: after each line sung by four of the voices, the fifth repeats the last word quite in the Gilbert and Sullivan manner, thus:

> 1st S.A.T.B. Dido, chi giace entro quest' urna?
> 2nd S. . . . . . Un urna!
> 1st S.A.T.B. Disse, chi sta sotto quel sasso?
> 2nd S. . . . . . Un sasso!

Before leaving the subject of the secular madrigals a final word must be spared for the six-part *Quando dal terzo cielo*, which appeared in a collection by various composers, entitled *Il trionfo di Dori*, printed at Venice in 1592. The poem eulogizes the 'fairest of all nymphs,' describing the welcome awaiting her in Arcadia—the shepherds' songs of greeting resounding through the air, the cries of 'Viva la bella Dori.' This pageant-like scene is reflected in music of genial charm and fancy: from the exquisite soaring phrase at the commencement (picturing the 'third heaven' whence Doris appears) to the end where the voices vie with one another in crying 'viva,' it moves along with something of the stateliness of a Milton ode.

In the spiritual madrigal Palestrina found an ideal medium for artistic expression within the smaller form—a field of poetry as vivid and expressive and imaginative as the secular, yet possessing a religious significance. Here his purely musical gift could have free play in the atmosphere most congenial to it.

In the two collections of *madrigali spirituali* published by the composer in 1581 and 1594 we find page after page of music, in turn meditative, mystic, impassioned, all tinged with an intimate beauty; we may not be far wrong in regarding it all as a musical mirror of the composer's own soul, a reflection of his inmost spiritual thoughts and aspirations.[1] In form and style these madrigals possess some of the attributes both of the

[1] Raugel speaks of the second book as 'le testament artistique du prenestin.'

motet and the secular madrigal; the thematic material is simple and the vocal parts move lightly and gracefully. The first few form a set by themselves, the texts being taken from Petrarch's *Vergine bella*, in which the poet extols the mystic graces of the Blessed Virgin. Each of these has a character differentiating it from all the others—the dignified music in which the 'Vergine bella . . . coronata di stelle' is depicted, the simple beauty of the 'Vergine pura,' the gracious charm expressive of the 'Vergine sola al mondo, senza esempio,' the limpid freshness one finds in 'Vergine chiara e stabile in eterno.'

Among the other madrigals are almost equally beautiful pieces. The Third Person of the Trinity is invoked in *Spirito Santo, Amore* and *Paraclito amoroso*, the first of these remarkable for music of quiet devotional character, lightening suddenly at the cry 'Signor, illustra il tenebroso core' and rising to an impassioned climax, inspired by the poetic imagery of 'O raggio procedente da le due eterne stelle' ('O ray from the two eternal stars proceeding'). Two Eucharistic meditations—*O cibo di dolcezza* and *O manna saporito*—have music of appropriate mystic quality, and two others, the beautiful prayer *O Jesu dolce* and *Amor, senza il tuo dono*, must claim places among the best of this first book.

The madrigals of the second (1591) book are not quite on the same musical level as those of the first, although a few are of the same fine quality. The subjects of the poems are the titles and attributes of the Blessed Virgin, some of which are recited in the litany of Loretto—such as Mirror of Justice, Tower of Ivory, Gate of Heaven, Mystic Rose, Queen of Virgins. They are all set in the same refined, elegant style, but in general the thematic ideas are not so distinctive, nor is their treatment so striking. The best of them are the motet-like *Regina delle vergini*, with its reminiscences of the plainchant *Regina coeli*; *E con i raggi tuoi*, where the music has a warmth and glow inspired by the words; *Dammi vermiglia rosa*; *Tu di fortezza torre*; *Vello di Giedeon* and *Se amarissimo fiele e tosco*, remarkable for its bold dissonances.[1]

In between the two books of *madrigali spirituali* Palestrina wrote a work which is generally acclaimed as a masterpiece— a setting of part of the *Canticle of Canticles*—although the musical world has neglected it to the extent that performances of the music seem almost unknown.[2] Palestrina may have been stimulated to the composition of this, as well as the spiritual madrigals, by the growing demand for such music. Under the leadership of St Philip Neri in Rome, and other saintly men elsewhere, a wave of religious revival was at that time spreading over Italy. This reawakening of spiritual life brought many reunions of orders, confraternities and congregations, at which it was usual to include music of a sacred character. Liturgical works were unsuitable, but the spiritual madrigal, where instead of the ecclesiastical Latin the vulgar tongue could be used in music praising the Saviour and the Blessed Virgin, seemed just what was needed. The various re-editions of the spiritual madrigals and the *Canticle of Canticles*[3] during the years following their appearance are a proof of how popular they soon became as adjuncts to the devotional exercises conducted by religious leaders.

The music of the last-named work represents Palestrina's highest achievement in the madrigal field. It is true that the composer himself described the movements as motets, but he had good reasons for avoiding the use of the term 'madrigal,'[4]

---

[1] Burney quotes a passage from this madrigal in his *History*.

[2] Since this was written the B.B.C. has broadcast the work.

[3] It is quite possible that this may also have been sung in the vernacular.

[4] See the preface to the first edition of the *Canticle of Canticles*, quoted in Chapter I, p. 4.

with which they have a far greater affinity. However, in setting to music the Song of Solomon Palestrina was, in fact, again making use of love poetry of the most impassioned kind; but here he was on safe ground, for the Canticle has always been used by the Catholic church, irrespective of its origin, as a symbolical illustration of 'the happy union of Christ and His Spouse. . . . The Spouse is the church, more especially as to the happiest part of it, namely perfect souls, every one of which is His beloved.'[1]

This, of course, was the view Palestrina would take; his music has a twofold aspect, presenting the secular picture and also reflecting the mystic-religious meaning of the words. There are twenty-nine short movements, the selection of the texts having been made with a view to affording the requisite variety and contrast, and also giving some sort of artistic coherence, for the music is to be regarded as a whole, not merely as a series of detached unrelated movements.

It has been said that here Palestrina exhibits an entirely new style, emotional and dramatic, foreign to the rest of his work. But a careful examination reveals the same artistic principles at work as in the masses and motets, the same impersonal style, the same concentration upon underlining the significance of the text. There is never any attempt at dramatizing the narrative, nor any idea of characterizing the chief personages—the Lover and the Beloved. Thus when the latter seeks her lover through the daughters of Jerusalem (*Adjuro vos, filiae Hierusalem*) not one voice, but all five, enter in turn with the entreaty. It is Palestrina's own way of giving impressive effect to the situation. The decorative element is employed, but with new skill, the pictorial method with more vividness, while the rhythmic variation is most subtle. How all this is linked

[1] The quotation is from Bishop Challoner's notes to the English version of the Latin Vulgate.

up with the rest of Palestrina's work one instance will serve to show. In the two movements beginning with the word 'surge' the composer actually employs the same figure, with hardly any alteration, as in the motet *Surge illuminare*. As an example of the rhythmic elasticity of the music this passage from *Dilectus meus mihi* may be quoted:

where several variants of the theme are woven together simultaneously.

The range of style the music shows is remarkable: the fresh-ness and warmth of the secular madrigals; the delicacy and refinement of the spiritual madrigals; even the more serious style of the motets—all are utilized to form that *genus aliquantum alacrius* which the composer himself declared he had em-ployed in this work, the character of which is in turn delicate, vivid, brilliant, simple, elaborate, faithfully reflecting the picture presented by the text in each case.

All the twenty-nine movements display a remarkable beauty and finish of workmanship, some of them possessing features or special interest. *Dilectus meus mihi*, from which a quotation has already been given, is full of delicate, melodious, gently moving music: the portrait of the Shulamite in *Nigra sum* is set to music with a suggestion of Oriental melody. *Quae est ista*, the words of which are also used in the liturgy, as symbolical of the Blessed Virgin, has some fine descriptive touches—a dreamy passage suggestive of 'pulchra ut luna,' the sudden brightening of the music a moment later, at the words 'electa ut sol,' the splendid vigour of 'castrorum acies ordinata' ('terrible as an army'), where a forceful *motif* strides about in the surging polyphony. The soft, berceuse-like rhythm and melody of *Laeva ejus*, picturing the Beloved's slumber, deserves a quotation:

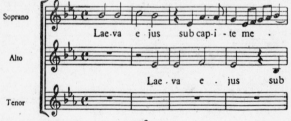

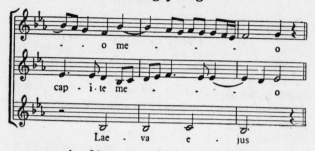

as an example of its grace and beauty. *Vox dilecti*, after an introduction which seems an evocation of the Beloved's voice echoing from afar, proceeds with a series of lively, curving figures evidently meant to portray the Lover, 'leaping upon the mountains, skipping upon the hills.' The music of *Veni dilecte mi* is full of tenderness and sweetness. *Introduxit me rex in cellam*, where the words 'quia amore langueo' are treated realistically, in tender, long-drawn-out phrases, is considered by some to be the finest movement in the work.

CHAPTER XII

MISCELLANEOUS WORKS

MORE than a century and a half ago Dr Burney called the attention of his countrymen to a then unknown musical master-piece—Palestrina's *Stabat Mater* for double choir (eight voices) —although the manner of his doing so was perhaps not particularly creditable. The work had been presented by the composer to the Papal Choir, by whom it was jealously guarded as an exclusive possession, to be performed by them alone, every Good Friday. Burney managed to get a copy of the music, apparently by bribing one of the singers, and published it in England, in 1771, together with other music sung during Holy Week at Rome.

For more than one reason, however, the *Stabat Mater* remained neglected here, in spite of Burney's panegyric: not until, with the dawn of the nineteenth century and the reawakening of musical culture by such men as Samuel Wesley (1766–1837), who thought almost as much of Palestrina as of his adored Bach, was there any sign of interest in the former's music; not until, in fact, Wesley's friend, Vincent Novello, began to publish some of the masses and motets. Even in our own time performances of the *Stabat Mater* are few and far between, although it is a work which should take its place beside the *Matthew Passion* with at least one yearly performance during the appropriate season.

The date of its composition is about 1589 or 1590; it belongs, therefore, to the last period. Outwardly it is one of the simplest of Palestrina's large-scale works. Here is no parade of musical ingenuity, no display of contrapuntal skill, no music for music's sake. Nevertheless, beneath this apparent simplicity lies concealed a subtle and studied sense of effect. As so often with

Palestrina, one realizes that the essential greatness of the music, its ageless quality, is due in part to the self-effacement of the musician, the concentration on bringing home to the listener the meaning and significance of the text, carrying out the composer's own maxim, 'dare spirito vivo alle parole.'

This very restraint helps to create the mystic devotional atmosphere of the music and to make its beauty all the more impressive, revealing, too, the delicate rhythmical nuances (unfortunately masked by the bar-lines in modern editions) so perfectly fitting the metrical accent of the words; the exquisite melodic contours; the superb harmonic effects, one of which, occurring at the very beginning, has already been quoted.[1]

The *Stabat Mater* falls into several divisions, although there is no actual break in the music. In the first part the constant antiphonal use of the two choirs may be intended to symbolize a dialogue between groups of pious folk who in imagination behold the sufferings of the Saviour on the cross, and the anguish of His Mother at witnessing those sufferings. The style here is mainly homophonic, and from time to time Palestrina has employed, with the same solemnly beautiful effect, a series of major triads, as for instance at the point where all the voices join in the cry of compassion, 'O quam tristis'; here seven successive major chords are heard. A *motif* of four descending notes also appears in the musical fabric from time to time; at the close of the work it is more prominent.

This first part ends with an exquisite cadence at the words announcing the death of the Redeemer: 'Dum emisit spiritum,' a new movement commencing with the invocation of the Mother, 'Eia Mater, fons amoris.' The music again resumes the antiphonal dialogue, while once more, as the two choirs join in the petition 'Sancta Mater, istud agas,' a majestic suc-cession of major chords is heard, with the same solemnly

[1] See Chapter VIII, p. 90.

beautiful effect as before. This is again repeated at the words 'Donec ego vixero,' leading to a third part. Here the music takes on a serene loveliness: the sopranos of each choir joins in a gentle melody in thirds, while a tenor theme moves lightly against this; the colour of the voices and the quiet movement of the polyphony combine to create a mood of tenderness in perfect keeping with the appeal to the Mother: 'Juxta crucem tecum stare.'

This central part of the work is succeeded by more antiphonal dialogue which gradually rises to a stately climax at the words 'ad palmam victoriae.' The short epilogue bringing the music to a close concludes with a sublimely beautiful passage, the voices softly echoing 'Paradisi' to the four-note *motif* mentioned above.

183

A setting of the *Stabat Mater* in twelve parts (three choirs of four voices each), included in the Breitkopf & Härtel edition, is often attributed to Palestrina's pupil Francesco Anerio. It has something of the style of the work just described, although it lacks its beauty and subtlety of nuance. But a curious fact is that we find the four-note theme quoted above utilized in it, and the same theme also appears in an unfinished setting, of doubtful authenticity, in four and eight parts.

When asked by the Società Musicale Romana, in 1880, to contribute a work for the unveiling of a bust of Palestrina, Wagner sent instead three of the composer's works—the *Stabat Mater,* the 'Sanctus' from the Mass *Aeterna Christi munera* and a Magnificat.[1] One does not know which of the thirty-five settings of the canticle composed by Palestrina was Wagner's choice—possibly the fine work in eight parts written for the Papal Choir. The Magnificats constitute a highly characteristic part of Palestrina's liturgical music and are specially interesting as examples of writing strictly in the modes. They are an illustration of the remark made in an earlier chapter, that music such as this has its roots in plainchant, for it grows out of the psalm tones to which the Magnificat is sung in plainchant.

Long before Palestrina's day there was a custom of adorning alternate verses of the plainchant with *faux-bourdons*. This plan forms the basis of the Palestrinian settings, where the alternate verses are treated in polyphony (for four, five or six voices), these contrapuntal themes being also founded upon the psalm tones, forming choral variations thereon.

There are four complete series of Magnificats upon each of the eight tones: two of these series Palestrina published in 1591; the others remained at his death in manuscripts belonging

[1] This story is vouched for by Raugel.

to the Julian Choir (of St Peter's) and to St John Lateran.
The eight-part Magnificat mentioned is on the first tone, and
two more exist on the fourth and fifth tones.

The composition of these thirty-five works was in all probability spread over a long period. Those belonging to the
Julian Choir are assumed to date from Palestrina's first stay at
St Peter's (1551-5), and those at St John Lateran to the corresponding period there (1555-60). While this is merely con-
jecture, the rather florid, ornate style of the music and the constant employment of ingenious canonic devices—two of them in
six parts on the fourth and fifth tones are particularly elaborate
—seems to point to the earlier dates. On the other hand, those
printed in 1591 were described by Palestrina himself (in the
preface dedicating them to Pope Gregory XIV) as recently
written ('nuper lucubratum'). We must not take this phrase
too literally—perhaps only in the comparative sense; nevertheless these particular Magnificats have an ease of movement
—homophony is almost entirely absent from them, by the way
—a melodic suavity, a clarity and that simplicity of effect
which Palestrina eventually realized as the most suitable for
church music, a style which, as already remarked, is shown
to perfection in such masses as *Aeterna Christi munera* and *Iste
confessor*. These Magnificats may therefore have been written
at about the same time, i.e. from 1575 to 1585.

In any case Palestrina probably had an eye to business in
selecting them for publication, as not being too elaborate (they
are in three and four parts) and consequently within the
capabilities of an average choir.

Viewing the Magnificats as a whole, one is struck by the
remarkable way in which he employs the same simple *motifs*
of the psalm tones not only over and over again in the same
work, but in a second, a third and even a fourth composition
upon the identical psalm tone. Yet each time he contrives to

evolve from it fresh and varied ideas. The manner in which the plainchant intonations are ornamented with decorative figures recalls Debussy's simile of 'scroll-like melodies,' for they certainly remind us of the embellishments of the capital letters in an old missal. Each part of the psalm tone generates contrapuntal melodies, thus:

an - cil-lae su - - - - - ae

mi - ser-i-cordi - ae su - - ae

The example is quoted from the beautiful Magnificat on the eighth tone, one of the best in the 1591 book. Here the two middle verses are set in lighter style, for three voices, and it may be that these were sung by solo singers in the composer's day. The same plan is followed in the other settings, and variety is obtained by treating the odd verses in one series, the even in the other.

The Julian Choir Magnificats are designed in the same way, in four parts, with a 'Gloria' for five or six voices. They are not of such distinction as those for the Lateran Choir: the latter are in five or six parts, an extra voice being added for the 'Gloria.' The best of them are a six-part work (third tone) and one in five parts on the first tone. The latter is particularly effective, especially because of the striking use made of the *motif* formed from the first four rising notes of the 'tone.' In these 'Lateran' Magnificats the first two verses are set (except for the liturgical intonation of the first word), leaving only the third, fifth and seventh to be sung in plainchant. The fourth and eighth verses in the first-tone setting just mentioned are beautifully written for four voices only, and here once more Palestrina's sense of tone-colour is in evidence—one verse is for two sopranos and two altos, the other assigned to two tenors and two basses.

In the eight-part Magnificat referred to above the whole of the canticle is set for two choirs, of four voices each. The music here is much freer in style, the outline of the psalm tone being only faintly discernible in the polyphony. Much of it is anti-phonal in style; the treatment of the verse 'Quia fecit mihi magna,' where the two soprano parts sing a melody in thirds, with accompanying counterpoints from alto and tenor, recalls the middle movement of the *Stabat Mater* and may perhaps be evidence of the two works having been written about the same time.

From a purely musical point of view the *Stabat Mater* must be considered the finest of the Holy Week compositions. Of the rest, the *Lamentations* (sung at the office of Tenebrae on Maundy Thursday, Good Friday and Holy Saturday) derive their artistic value to a great degree from their perfect appropriateness to the liturgical requirements, making the music almost an integral part of the rite itself. Nevertheless there are many passages of purely musical charm—exquisite bits where the voices are woven in counterpoint or sung in impressively beautiful harmonies.

The *Lamentations* consist of nine lessons, three for Tenebrae on each day. Palestrina, with his usual prodigality, set them four times over, publishing, however, only one version, in 1588. The other settings, unprinted for centuries after, are to be found in the choir-books of the papal chapel, the Julian chapel and St John Lateran.

As with the Magnificats, Palestrina chose to publish the simplest of these settings, and doubtless for the same reasons—suitability and practicability. They were probably the last to be written, for the more elaborate versions belonging to the choirs mentioned date as we know from earlier years. Those for the Papal Choir seem to have been composed, at the request of Pope Gregory XIII, in 1574, the Julian Choir music apparently a year later. In all these three the voices employed vary from three to eight, and in their combination and contrast we note once more that keen sense of tone-colour Palestrina possessed.

Mendelssohn, as we have seen, criticized Palestrina for setting to music the preliminary 'Incipit Lamentatio [or De Lamentatione] Jeremiae Prophetae,' and the Hebrew letters (Aleph, Heth, Gimel, etc.) denoting the commencement of the verses. But we ought rather to admire the way in which, for the furtherance of his artistic ends, the composer utilized them as part of his design, treating the sentences as preludes, while the initial letters take the place of what, in a later period, would have been short instrumental interludes between the vocal movements. And in pursuance of this scheme, it may be pointed out, these 'preludes' and 'interludes' are set to a quiet polyphony, in contrast to the text, where the music is generally homophonic. Indeed, these 'instrumental' portions of the *Lamentations* contain some of the finest music, particularly the 'letters,' which in themselves are miniature lamentations, built up in each case from a 'wailing' *motif*. Here is a particularly beautiful example from the second lesson of the Good Friday Tenebrae:

In every case the contrapuntal themes for these 'letters' are derived from this simple plainsong figure:

and we cannot but admire the apparently inexhaustible fertility and the resource shown in evolving new themes therefrom. The simple music of the lessons themselves is often founded upon the original plainchant and also, in some cases, the music of the exhortation that closes each lesson—'Jerusalem, Jerusalem, convertere ad Dominum Deum tuum.' The pathos with which Palestrina has, time after time, invested this appeal is really remarkable, the more so because so often the effects are produced with quite simple means, as, for example, in this excerpt from one of the 1588 lessons:

*G

The words, indeed, have inspired several passages of uncommon beauty: in the St John Lateran *Lamentations* there is a magnificent eight-part movement which, as one writer suggests, might well serve for a picture of the Jewish people mourning their captivity.

In these particular *Lamentations* there is much fine music of sombre beauty, the effect of which is heightened by the use of men's voices only. Possibly they owe something of this quality to the dark days through which Rome passed at the time of their composition.

Brief mention only can be made of the litanies which appeared in 1593. They are settings of various devotions, now obsolete, which at that time were used by the Confraternities of the Rosary.[1] Six of them are addressed to the Blessed Virgin, another is a Eucharistic litany, the last a litany to Our Lord. Their music is of simple devotional character, mostly homophonic, with the melodic phrases chiefly in the upper part; there are two sets of five each, all in four-part form: the second set is written for alto, two tenors and bass, the alto part being a kind of *obbligato* which, the composer indicates, may be omitted, so that the litanies are available for men's voices only, in three parts.

If we reject the authenticity of the organ *ricercari*, eight move-

---

[1] Their use was discontinued early in the following century by the pope's order, and superseded by the litany of Loretto.

ments written upon the Gregorian 'tones'—pleasant little pieces, but not in any way revealing the master hand—Palestrina wrote no instrumental music of any kind. Yet he began his career as an organist, and we know he could play the lute, while later in life, at the Villa d' Este, he was in charge of a small orchestra, something like the one he has pictured so delightfully in the motet *Exultate Deo*; yet neither the keyboard nor the wind and string instruments seem to have attracted him as a composer.

One obvious explanation of this lies in the fact that, at the middle of the sixteenth century, instrumental music was in a comparatively undeveloped state (due in part to the technical limitations of instruments) as compared with the high degree of perfection attained in vocal art. An account of a type of organ in use about the middle of the sixteenth century has been given on a previous page: there were bigger instruments, of course, but their artistic qualities were probably very limited, although improvements were being rapidly made towards the end of Palestrina's life.

In Banchieri's *L' organo suonarino*, published in 1605, one may find organ music written on three staves, i.e. with a simple independent pedal part, and such little pieces as this and other publications of about the same date contain show a style of Italian organ music in process of development. Had Palestrina lived a little longer and, in accordance with his intention, in semi-retirement as organist of St Agapit's in his native city, it is quite likely he might have composed some organ music for church use. But in the full tide of his active creative career neither organ or orchestra could offer him the sonority and the shading of colour that his music required. And over and above all this was the knowledge and conviction that his great gift was destined to serve the church which had nurtured, even inspired it. In fulfilling that destiny his creative powers found their greatest and most perfect expression.

APPENDICES

APPENDIX A

CALENDAR

(Figures in brackets denote the age reached by the person mentioned during the year in question.)

Year	Approx. Age	Life	Contemporary Musicians
1525 (?)		Giovanni Pierluigi born, (?) Dec. 17, at Palestrina, in the Sabine Hills, son of Sante Pierluigi, a citizen in comfortable circumstances.	Brumel (*c.* 65) dies; Farrant born (approx.); Goudimel born (approx.). Animuccia aged *c.* 25; Arcadelt *c.* 11; Buus *c.* 10; Cabezon 15; Certon *c.* 30; Clement *c.* 51; Corteccia *c.* 20; Crequillon *c.* 15; Dietrich *c.* 34; Ducis *c.* 45; Festa *c.* 30; Finck (Heinrich) *c.* 60; Gabrieli (Andrea) *c.* 15; Genet *c.* 55; Gombert *c.* 20; Guerrero *c.* 7; Hellinck *c.* 65; Hofhaimer 66; Jachet *c.* 20; Jannequin *c.* 20; Johnson (Robert) *c.* 35; Mel *c.* 5; Merbecke *c.* 10; de Monte *c.* 3; Morales *c.* 25; Ortiz *c.* 15; Paminger 30; Pygott *c.* 30; Redford *c.* 40; Richafort *c.* 25; Rore *c.* 9; Ruffo *c.* 5; Scandello

Year	Approx. Age	Life	Contemporary Musicians
			8; Senfl *c.* 45; Sermisy *c.* 35; Shepherd *c.* 15; Tallis *c.* 20; Taverner *c.* 30; Tye *c.* 25; Vaet *c.* 5; Verdelot *c.* 25; Waelrant *c.* 7; Walther (Johann) 29; Wannenmacher *c.* 40; Willaert *c.* 45.
1526	1		
1527	2	During the sacking of Rome by the Emperor Charles V (27), the town of Palestrina is partly destroyed and many inhabitants are killed. P. and his family are spared. The town archives, probably containing date of P.'s birth, burnt.	Annibale born (approx.); Finck (Heinrich) (*c.* 62) dies, June 9; Finck (Hermann) born, March 21.
1528	3		
1529	4		
1530	5		Donati born (approx.); Lassus born (approx.); Navarro born (approx.); Porta born (approx.); Whyte born (approx.).
1531	6		Costeley born.
1532	7	(?) Becomes chorister in the cathedral of St Agapit at Palestrina (approx.).	Guidetti born.
1533	8		Merulo born, *c.* April.
1534	9	Cardinal Andrea della Valle, Bishop of Palestrina, made arch-priest of	

Year	Approx. Age	Life	Contemporary Musicians
		Santa Maria Maggiore in Rome. Takes P. with him and enters him in the choir school.	
1535	10		Genet (*c.* 65) dies (approx.); Ingegneri born (approx.); Striggio born (approx.); Victoria born (approx.).
1536	11		de Wert born (approx.).
1537	12	P.'s name occurs in a chapter minute as one of the elder choirboys.	
1538	13		
1539	14	P. leaves the choir, his voice having broken, and returns home for a short time.	Hofhaimer (80) dies.
1540	15	(?) Returns to Rome. Firmin Le Bel becomes *maestro di cappella* at Santa Maria Maggiore and P. probably studies under him.	Ferrabosco (i) born (approx.); Le Jeune born (approx.); Schroeter born (approx.); Pinello di Gherardi born (approx.).
1541	16		Hellinck (*c.* 81) dies (approx.).
1542	17		Meiland born (approx.).
1543	18		Byrd born; Pevernage born; Regnart born (approx.).
1544	19	Appointed organist and *maestro di canto* at the cathedral of St Agapit at his native town, Palestrina,	

Year	Approx. Age	Life	Contemporary Musicians
		under Bishop Cardinal Giovanni del Monte (67). He leaves Rome.	
1545	20	His duties at the cathedral of St Agapit involve instruction of the canons and boys, and organ playing on festival days.	Balbi born (approx.); Festa (*c.* 50) dies, April 10; Gastoldi born (approx.); Lechner born (approx.); Luzzaschi born (approx.); Nanini (G. M.) born (approx.); Redford (*c.* 60) dies; Regnart (J.) born (approx.); Taverner (*c.* 50) dies.
1546	21		
1547	22	Marries Lucrezia Gori, June 12. His wife inherits a vineyard, fields, household goods and a sum of money after the death of her father, Francesco Gori, Nov.	
1548	23		Dietrich (*c.* 57) dies.
1549	24	Birth of P.'s eldest son Rodolfo.	du Caurroy born; Soriano born.
1550	25	Accession of Cardinal del Monte (73) to the papal chair as Julius III.	Asola born (approx.); Baccusi born (approx.); Cavalieri born (approx.); Ducis (*c.* 70) dies; Handl born (approx.); Johnson (Edward) born (approx.); Mancinus born; Vecchi born.
1551	26	Birth of P.'s second son,	Richafort (*c.* 51) dies (ap-

Year	Approx. Age	Life	Contemporary Musicians
		Angelo. Is appointed *maestro di cappella* of the Julian Choir at St Peter's in Rome by Pope Julius III (74).	prox.); Wannenmacher (*c.* 66) dies (approx.).
1552	27		
1553	28		Eccard born; Morales (*c.* 53) dies; Pygott (*c.* 58) dies (approx.).
1554	29	Madrigal, *Con dolce, altiero*, published in Gardano's fourth book of madrigals in Venice. First book of masses published by Valerio and Aloisio Dorico and dedicated to Pope Julius III (77).	
1555	30	Julius III (78) makes P. a member of the Pontifical Choir without an entrance examination, Jan. The members resent his presence for that reason and because he has a poor voice. Death of Julius III, March 23, and accession of Marcellus II (54), April 9. The new pope intends to reform the church music. He addresses the papal singers on Good Friday, criticizing the style of performance. He dies, May 1.	Leoni born (approx.); Senfl (*c.* 75) dies (approx.).

197

Year	Approx. Age	Life	Contemporary Musicians
		Accession of Paul IV (79), May 23. P., with others, is retired on pension from the Pontifical Choir by the new pope, May. P. has a serious illness, July. The chapter appoints him *maestro di cappella* at San Giovanni in Laterano, Oct. 1. (?) First book of madrigals published.	
1556	31		Calvisius born, Feb. 21.
1557	32	Canzone for 4 voices contributed to Cyprian de Rore's (c. 41) second book of madrigals.	Clement (c. 83) dies (approx.); Croce born (approx.); Gabrieli (Giovanni) born; Gesualdo, Prince of Venosa, born (approx.); Mauduit born, Sept. 16; Morley born.
1558	33		Caccini born (approx.); Finck (Hermann) (31) dies, Dec. 28.
1559	34	Death of Pope Paul IV (83) and accession of Cardinal Giovanni Angelo de' Medici (60) as Pius IV.	Jachet (c. 54) dies.
1560	35	The chapter of St John Lateran decides to effect some economies in the management of the choir, July. P. resigns his appointment of *maestro di cappella*, Aug.	Belli (Girolamo) born (approx.); Cobbold born, Jan. 5; Crequillon (c. 50) dies (approx.); Diruta born (approx.); Giovanelli born; Gombert (c. 55) dies (approx.); Gumpeltzhaimer born (approx.); Jannequin

Year	Approx. Age	Life	Contemporary Musicians
			(*c.* 85) dies (approx.); Marenzio born (approx.); Nanini (G. B.) born (approx.); Pallavicino born (approx.); Philips born (approx.); Praetorius (Hieronymus) born, Aug. 10; Quagliati born (approx.); Raval born (approx.); Rossi (Salomone) born (approx.).
1561	36	Is appointed *maestro di cappella* at Santa Maria Maggiore, March 1. Third son, Iginio, born (approx.).	Peri born, Aug. 20.
1562	37		Belli (Giulio) born (approx.); Bull born; Dulichius born; Sermisy (*c.* 72) dies; Sweelinck born; Willaert (*c.* 82) dies, Dec. 7.
1563	38	First book of motets published and dedicated to Cardinal Rodolfo Pio di Carpi, Bishop of Ostia. At the twentyfourth meeting of the Council of Trent, Nov. 11, the question of the reform of church music is discussed.	Dowland born; Raselius born (approx.); Shepherd (*c.* 53) dies (approx.); Verdonck born.
1564	39	P. obtains leave and goes into the service of Cardinal Ippolito d' Este for the summer.	Hassler born; Viadana born (approx.).

Year	Approx. Age	Life	Contemporary Musicians
1565	40	Death of Pope Pius IV (66). P. appointed director of the newly established Roman seminary. His sons Angelo and Rodolfo become scholars there.	Aichinger born; Anerio (Felice) born (approx.); Farmer born (approx.); Guédron born (approx.); Johnson (Robert) (*c.* 75) dies (approx.); Kirbye born (approx.); Mundy born (approx.); Pilkington born (approx.); Rore (*c.* 49) dies, autumn.
1566	41	Accession of Michele Ghislieri (62) as Pius V, Jan. 7.	Cabezon (56) dies, March 26; Ortiz (*c.* 56) dies (approx.); Verdelot (*c.* 66) dies (approx.).
1567	42	Vol. II of masses published and dedicated to Philip II of Spain (40). P. gives up his appointment at Santa Maria Maggiore, beginning of year, and officiates at St John Lateran during Holy Week. He continues in the service of Cardinal Ippolito d' Este (?).	Anerio (Giovanni Francesco) born (approx.); Banchieri born (approx.); Monteverdi born, May; Paminger (72) dies, May 3; Vaet (*c.* 47) dies, Jan. 8.
1568	43	Emperor Maximilian offers P. a post as musical director at his Viennese court. P.'s terms rejected as too high. P. corresponds with Guglielmo Gonzaga, Duke of Mantua, who, through de Wert (*c.* 32), who is in his service, re-	Comes born; Farnaby born (approx.).

Year	Approx. Age	Life	Contemporary Musicians
		quests P. to write a mass for the church of Santa Barbara built by him, Feb. P. sends motets set to words by the duke to Mantua. P. has serious illness, Dec.	
1569	44	First book of five-part motets published by Scoto of Venice and dedicated to Cardinal Ippolito d' Este, in whose service he still remains.	
1570	45	Third book of masses published and dedicated to Philip II of Spain (43). P. returns a madrigal and a motet by Duke Guglielmo Gonzaga to Mantua with his corrections, March 23.	Coperario (Cooper) born (approx.); Dering born (approx.); Jones (Robert) born (approx.); Pacelli born (approx.); Walther (Johann) (74) dies.
1571	46	Madrigal, *Le selv' avea*, composed to celebrate the victory of Lepanto and especially Marc' Antonio Colonna, P.'s property at Palestrina being lorded over by the Colonna family.	Animuccia (*c.* 71) dies, March; Corteccia (*c.* 66) dies, June 7; Praetorius (Michael) born, Feb. 15.
1572	47	Guglielmo Gonzaga, Duke of Mantua, visits Rome. Vol. II of motets in five to eight parts, published by Scoto of Venice, is dedicated to him. Death of	Goudimel (*c.* 47) dies, Aug. 27.

Year	Approx. Age	Life	Contemporary Musicians
		Pius V (68), May 1, and accession of Ugo Buoncompagno (70) as Pope Gregory XIII. Death of P.'s patron, Cardinal Ippolito d' Este, and of his son Rodolfo (*c.* 22), end of year.	
1573	48	P.'s brother, Silla Pierluigi, dies, Jan. P. is obliged to excuse himself for not carrying out a commission from Guglielmo Gonzaga, Duke of Mantua, owing to illness. P.'s second son, Angelo, married.	Franck (Melchior) born (approx.); Pujol born; Tomkins born; Tye (73) dies, March 15.
1574	49	Set of *Lamentations* composed by desire of Gregory XIII (72).	Besler born, Dec. 15; Wilbye born, March.
1575	50	The chapter of Santa Maria Maggiore endeavours to induce P. to return into the service of that church by offering him a larger salary than he receives at St Peter's; but he persuades the latter to increase his pay and remains. Vol. III of motets published and dedicated to Alfonso d' Este, Duke of Ferrara (42). Death of P.'s son Angelo (*c.* 21), Dec.	Arcadelt (*c.* 61) dies (approx.); Bateson born (approx.); Campion born; Cifra born (approx.); Ferrabosco (ii) born (approx.); Gagliano born (approx.); Grandi born (approx.); Micheli born (approx.); Rosseter born (approx.); Weelkes born (approx.).

Year	Approx. Age	Life	Contemporary Musicians
1576	51	Marriage of P.'s youngest and only surviving son, Iginio (*c.* 16), to Virginia Guarnecci.	
1577	52	Gregory XIII (75) issues a decree for the revision of the Gradual, a task P. and Annibale Zoilo are directed to carry out.	Meiland (*c.* 35) dies.
1578	53		Agazzari born, Dec. 2.
1579	54		
1580	55	Death of P.'s wife, Lucrezia, July. P. applies to Pope Gregory XIII to be admitted to the priesthood, Nov. Takes the preliminary step, entering the 'clerical state' on receiving the first tonsure at St Sylvester on the Quirinal, Dec. Motets, *Surge sancte Dei* and *Ambula sancte Dei*, composed for the transference of the relics of St Gregory.	Allegri born (approx.); Farrant (*c.* 55) dies; Ford born (approx.); Scandello (63) dies, Jan. 18; Stobaeus born, July 6.
1581	56	Appointed to vacant canonry at Ferrentina Cathedral, Jan. Leaves the clerical state and marries again, March 28, his second wife being Virginia Dormuli, the widow of a prosperous furrier. P. takes a partner	

Year	Approx. Age	Life	Contemporary Musicians
		and runs the furrier's business. Second book of motets for 4 voices and Vol. I of *Madrigali spirituali* published and dedicated to the Duke of Sora.	
1582	57	Vol. IV of masses published by Gardano of Venice and dedicated to Pope Gregory XIII (80). The *Directorium chori*, revised by P., Zoilo and Guidetti (50), published with a preface by P.	
1583	58	Duke of Mantua, wishing to engage a new musical director, asks P. to recommend one. Eventually P. suggests himself, but his terms are too high and the matter is dropped. Formation of the 'Company of Rome,' a union of native musicians which opposes the settlement of foreign musicians in Rome and especially in the Pontifical Choir.	Frescobaldi born; Gibbons born; Johnson (Robert ii) born (approx.); Lawes (William) born (approx.).
1584	59	Vol. IV of motets for five voices, to words from the Song of Solomon, published and dedicated to Pope Gregory XIII (82). Vol. V of motets for five	

Year	Approx. Age	Life	Contemporary Musicians
		voices published and dedicated to Prince Andrea Bathory, nephew of King Stephen of Poland (51).	
1585	60	Death of Pope Gregory XIII (83) and accession of Cardinal Felice Peretti (64) as Sixtus V, April. Two madrigals, *Vestiva i colli* and *Così le chiome mie*, published in the collection, *Spoglia amorosa*, by Scotto of Venice. An intrigue to appoint P. *maestro di cappella* of the Pontifical Choir is defeated, May. Sixtus V revises the constitution of the Papal Choir, Dec.	Merbecke (*c.* 70) dies (approx.); Schütz born, Oct. 8; Tallis (*c.* 80) dies, Nov. 23; Valentini born (approx.).
1586	61	The pope has the Egyptian obelisk set up in the piazza in front of St Peter's and P.'s setting of the hymn, *Vexilla Regis*, is sung. Vol. II of madrigals for four voices published.	Gabrieli (Andrea) (*c.* 76) dies; Schein born, Jan. 20.
1587	62	Death of Guglielmo Gonzaga, Duke of Mantua, with whom P. has remained in correspondence.	Pinello di Gherardi (*c.* 47) dies, June 15; Scheidt born; Striggio (*c.* 53) dies (approx.).
1588	63	Writes new *Lamentations* for Holy Week. They are published and dedicated to Sixtus V (67). Some of	Ferrabosco (i) (*c.* 48) dies; Herbst born; Lanier born, Aug. or Sept.

Year	Approx. Age	*Life*	*Contemporary Musicians*
		P.'s madrigals printed in England by East.	
1589	64	The 'Company of Rome' issues a collection of madrigals, *Le gioie*, edited by Felice Anerio (*c.* 24), its *maestro di cappella*, and containing pieces by P., Marenzio (*c.* 29), Giovanelli (29) and others. Harmonized version by P. of the Latin hymnal for four voices for the whole ecclesiastical year published.	
1590	65	Sixtus V (69) dies in Aug. Election of Giovanni Battista Castagna (69) as Urban VII, who dies Sept. 27. The new building of St Peter's, though unfinished, is now ready for use. Accession of Cardinal Nicolò Sfondrato (55) as Pope Gregory XIV, Dec. 5. Vol. V of masses published by Coattino of Rome and dedicated to William, Duke of Bavaria.	Aguilera de Heredia born (approx.); Merula born (approx.); Ravenscroft born (approx.); Ruffo (*c.* 70) dies (approx.); Sabbatini (Galeazzo) born (approx.); Vitali born (approx.).
1591	66	Set of Magnificats published and dedicated to Pope Gregory XIV (56), who dies Oct. 15. Accession of Cardinal Giovanni	Handl (*c.* 41) dies, July 18.

Year	Approx. Age	Life	Contemporary Musicians
		Antonio Fachinetti (72) as Innocent IX, Oct. 29. He dies Dec. 30.	
1592	67	Accession of Cardinal Ippolito Aldobrandini (57) as Clement VIII, Jan. 30. Madrigal, *Quando dal terzo cielo*, contributed to Gardano's collection, *Il trionfo di Dori*. Collection of psalms, *Psalmodia vespertina*, dedicated to P. by fourteen composers.	Guidetti (60) dies, Nov. 30; Ingegneri (*c.* 57) dies; Jenkins born.
1593	68	Set of Offertories and two books of Litanies published, the former dedicated to the Abbé de la Baume, a French patron of P.'s. P. seems to contemplate retiring from Rome to Palestrina, and promises the chapter of St Agapit's to take up the post of organist there temporarily. Prepares to go there early next year.	Agostini born.
1594	69	Dedication of Vol. VI of masses to Cardinal Pietro Aldobrandini, nephew of Pope Clement VIII (59). Vol. II of *Madrigali spirituali* dedicated to the wife of Ferdinando de' Medici (45), Grand Duke of Tus-	Lassus (*c.* 64) dies, June 14. Agazzari aged 16; Agostini 1; Aguilera de Heredia *c.* 4; Aichinger 29; Allegri *c.* 14; Anerio (F.) *c.* 29; Anerio (G. F.) *c.* 27; Annibale *c.* 67; Asola

cany. While Vol. VII of masses is being sent to press, P. is seized with a sudden illness, Jan. 26. Palestrina dies in Rome, Feb. 2, and is buried in the Cappella Nuova of old St Peter's.

c. 44; Baccusi c. 44; Balbi c. 49; Banchieri c. 27; Belli (Girolamo) c. 32; Belli (Giulio) c. 34; Besler 20; Bull 32; Byrd 51; Caccini c. 36; Calvisius 38; Campion 19; du Caurroy 45; Cavalieri c. 44; Cifra c. 19; Cobbold 34; Comes 26; Coperario (Cooper) c. 24; Costeley 63; Croce c. 37; Dering c. 24; Diruta c. 34; Donati c. 64; Dowland 31; Dulichius 32; Eccard 41; Farmer c. 29; Farnaby c. 26; Ferrabosco (ii) c. 19; Ford c. 14; Franck c. 21; Frescobaldi 11; Gabrieli (G.) 37; Gagliano c. 19; Gastoldi c. 49; Gesualdo c. 37; Gibbons 11; Giovanelli 34; Grandi c. 19; Guédron c. 29; Guerrero c. 76; Gumpeltzhaimer c. 34; Hassler 30; Herbst 6; Jenkins 2; Johnson (Edward) c. 34; Johnson (Robert ii) c. 11; Jones (Robert) c. 24; Kirbye c. 29; Lanier 6; Lawes (William) c. 11; Lechner c. 49; Le Jeune c. 54; Leoni c. 39; Luzzaschi

Year	Approx. Age	Life	Contemporary Musicians

c. 49; Mancinus 44; Marenzio *c.* 34; Mauduit 37; Mel *c.* 74; Merula *c.* 4; Merulo 61; Micheli *c.* 19; de Monte *c.* 72; Monteverdi 27; Morley 37; Mundy *c.* 29; Nanini (G. M.) *c.* 49; Nanini (G. B.) *c.* 34; Navarro *c.* 64; Pacelli *c.* 24; Pallavicini *c.* 34; Peri 33; Philips *c.* 34; Pilkington *c.* 29; Porta *c.* 64; Praetorius (H.) 34; Praetorius (M.) 23; Pujol 21; Quagliati *c.* 34; Raval *c.* 34; Ravenscroft *c.* 4; Raselius *c.* 31; Regnart (F.) *c.* 51; Regnart (J.) *c.* 49; Rosseter *c.* 19; Rossi (S.) *c.* 34; Sabbatini (G.) *c.* 4; Scheidt 7; Schein 8; Schroeter *c.* 54; Schütz 9; Soriano 45; Stobaeus 14; Sweelinck 32; Tomkins 21; Valentini *c.* 9; Vecchi 44; Verdonck 31; Viadana *c.* 30; Victoria *c.* 59; Vitali *c.* 4; Waelrant *c.* 76; Weelkes *c.* 19; Wert *c.* 58; Wilbye 20.

APPENDIX B

CATALOGUE OF WORKS

(The numbers in brackets refer to the volume of the complete edition in which the work mentioned is to be found.)

MASSES FOR FOUR VOICES

Aeterna Christi munera (14).
Ave Maria (16).
Ave Regina coelorum (18).
Descendit angelus Domini (20).
Dies sanctificatus (15).
Dum esset summus pontifex (17).
Ecce sacerdos magnus (10).
Emendemus (16).
Gabriel archangelus (10).
Già fu chi m' ebbe cara (19).
In illo tempore (19).
In majoribus duplicibus (23).
In minoribus duplicibus (23).
In te Domine speravi (15).
Inviolata (11).
Iste confessor (14).
Jam Christus astra ascenderat (14).
Missa ad fugam (11).
Missa brevis (12).
Missa de beata Virgine (11).
Missa de feria (12).
Missa prima (Lauda Sion) (13).
Missa primi toni (Io mi son giovinetta) (12).

(5).

Deo (5).
Numquid Sion dicet (5).
a (7).
s).
(5).
cit (5).
e. Anima mea turbata (5).
tyr (5).
Maria (5).
).
Christo infantes (7).
Deum (5).
ancti (5).
discipulis (5).
tephanum (5).
Salvatorem (5).
variis linguis (5).
reditatis mysterium (5).
nctus Paulus (5).
ei Deus (30).
rodes spiculatore (5).
s tua (5).
deris peccata mea, Domine (7).
em gloriari (5).
suavis est (30).
tus luctus (5).
gloriae (5).
ps gloriosissime Michael Archangele (7).
Hebraeorum (5).
est ista (5).
m pulchri sunt (5).
vidisti me Thoma (5).
ator mundi salva nos (5).
ve Regina. Eia ergo advocata nostra (5).

Missa quarta (13).
Missa secunda (primi toni) (13).
Missa sine nomine (11).
Missa sine nomine (15).
Missa tertia (Jesu, nostra redemptio) (13).
O Regem coeli (10).
O Rex gloriae (21).
Panis quem ego dabo (14).
Pater noster (24).
Quam pulchra es (15).
Quem dicunt homines (17).
Regina coeli (21).
Sanctorum meritis (16).
Spem in alium (12).
Veni sponsa Christi (18).
Virtute magna (10).

MASSES FOR FIVE VOICES

Ad coenam Agni (10).
Ascendo ad Patrem (21).
Aspice Domine (11).
Beatus Laurentius (23).
Dilexi quoniam (15).
L'homme armé (12).
Memor esto (17).
Missa prima (Eripe me de inimicis) (13)
Missa secunda (13).
Missa sine nomine (18).
Missa sine titulo (30)
Missa tertia (O magnum mysterium) (13).
Nigra sum (14).
O admirabile commercium (17).
O sacrum convivium (23).
O Virgo simul et Mater (19).

Panem nostrum (24).
Petra sancta (19).
Pro defunctis (10).
Qual è il più grand' amor? (21).
Quando lieta sperai (20).
Regina coeli (20).
Repleatur os meum (12).
Sacerdos et Pontifex (16).
Salve Regina (24).
Salvum me fac (11).
Sicut lilium inter spinas (14).
Tu es pastor ovium (16).
Vestiva i colli (18).

MASSES FOR SIX VOICES

Alma Redemptoris (20).
Assumpta est Maria (23).
Ave Maria (15).
Dum complerentur (17).
Ecce ego Joannes (24).
Illumina oculos meos (19).
In te Domine speravi (18).
Missa de beata Virgine (vel donninicalis) (12).
Missa octavi toni (20).
Missa Papae Marcelli (11).
Missa quinti toni (19).
Missa sine nomine (10).
Missa sine titulo (24).
Missa sine titulo (32).
Nasce la gioia mia (14).
Sacerdotes Domini (17).
Te Deum laudamus (18).
Tu es Petrus (21).
Tu es Petrus (24).

Ut, Re, M
Veni Creato
Viri Galilaei

Confitebor tibi Do
Fratres ego enim ac
Hodie Christus natu
Laudate Dominum om

Mo
(Se

Ad Dominum cum tribulare
Adoramus te, Christe (5).
Ad te levavi oculos meos.   M
Alma Redemptoris Mater.   T
Ascendens Christus in altum (7
Ave Maria gratia plena (5).
Ave Regina coelorum.   Gaude gl
Beatus Laurentius (5).
Beatus vir qui suffert (5).
Benedicta sit sancta Trinitas (5).
Benedictus Dominus Deus (30).
Confitemini Domino (5).
Congratulamini mihi omnes (5).
Deus, qui animae famuli tui Gregorii (7).
Dies sanctificatus (5).
Doctor bonus (5).
Domine quando veneris.   Commissa mea (5)
Domine, secundum actum meum (7).
Dum aurora finem daret (5).
Ecce nunc benedicite Dominum (5).
Ecce nunc benedicite Dominum (7).

Ego sum panis vivus
Exaudi Domine (5)
Fuit homo missus a
Fundamenta ejus.
Gaude Barbara bea
Gaudent in coelis
Gloriosi principes
Haec dies quam f
Heu mihi Domin
Hic est vere ma
Hodie beata virg
In diebus illis (
Innocentes pro
Iste est qui an
Isti sunt viri s
Jesus junxit S
Lapidabant S
Lauda Sion
Loquebantur
Magnus ba
Magnus sa
Miserere
Missa He
Nativitat
Ne recor
Nos aut
O quam
O quan
O Re
Prince
Pueri
Qua
Qua
Qu
Sal
Sa

Sicut cervus desiderat. Sitivit anima mea (5).
Sub tuum praesidium (5).
Super flumina Babylonis (5).
Surge, propera amica mea (5).
Surrexit pastor bonus (5).
Tollite jugum meum (5).
Tribus miraculis (5).
Tu es pastor ovium (5).
Valde honorandus est (5).
Veni sponsa Christi (5).

MOTETS FOR FIVE VOICES

Adjuro vos, filiae Hierusalem (4).* [1]
Aegypte noli flere (4).
Alleluia! tulerunt Dominum (1).
Angelus Domini descendit de coelo. Et introeuntes in monumentum (3).
Apparuit caro suo (4).
Ardens est cor meum (4).
Ascendo ad patrem meum. Ego rogabo patrem (2).
Ave Maria (3).
Ave Regina coelorum (4).
Ave Trinitatis sanctuarium (4).
Beatae Mariae Magdalenae (1).
Beatus Laurentius orabat (1).
Canite tuba in Sion. Rorate coeli (2).
Cantantibus organis. Biduanis ac triduanis (3).
Caput ejus aurum optimum (4).*
Caro mea vere est cibus (3).
Coenantibus illis accepit Jesus (2).
Congrega, Domine. Afflige opprimentes nos (3).
Corona aurea. Domine praevenisti eum (2).
Crucem sanctam subiit (1).

---

[1] The motets marked * constitute the cycle of twenty-nine settings from the Song of Solomon.

Cum pervenisset beatus Andreas (1).
Derelinquat impius viam (2).
Descendi in hortum meum (4).*
Deus qui dedisti legem (1).
Dilectus meus descendit in hortum suum (4).*
Dilectus meus mihi et ego illi (4).*
Domine Deus, qui conteris. Tu Domine (3).
Domine secundum actum meum (4).
Dominus Jesus in qua nocte (2).
Duo ubera tua (4).*
Ecce merces sanctorum (4).
Ecce tu pulcher es, dilecte mi (4).*
Ego sum panis vivus. Panis quem ego dabo (1).
Exi cito in plateas (2).
Exultate Deo (4).
Fasciculus myrrhae (4).*
Fuit homo missus a Deo. Erat Joannes in deserto (3).
Gaude Barbara beata. Gaude quia meruisti (2).
Gaude gloriosa (4).
Guttur tuum sicut (4).*
Hic est discipulus ille (1).
Hodie nata est beata Virgo (1).
Homo quidam fuit (2).
Inclytae sanctae virginis Catherinae (3).
In illo tempore egressus (2).
Introduxit me rex in cellam (4).*
Jubilate Deo, omnis terra. Laudate nomen ejus (3).
Laetus Hyperboream. O patruo pariterque (4).
Laeva ejus sub capite meo (4).*
Lapidabant Stephanum (1).
Manifesto vobis veritatem. Pax vobis, noli timere (3).
Memor esto verbi tui servo tuo (2).
Nigra sum, sed formosa (4).*
O admirabile commercium (1).
O Antoni eremita (1).
O beata et gloriosa Trinitas. O vera summa sempiterna Trinitas (1).

O beatum pontificem (1).
O beatum virum (1).
O lux et decus. O singulare praesidium (3).
Omnipotens sempiterne Deus (3).
O quam metuendus (3).
Orietur stella (4).
O sacrum convivium (2).
O sancte praesul Nicolae. Gaude praesul optime (3).
Osculetur me osculo oris sui (4).*
O Virgo simul et Mater (2).
Parce mihi Domine. Peccavi, peccavi (4).
Pater noster (3).
Paucitas dierum meorum. Manus tuae Domine (4).
Peccantem me quotidie (2).
Puer qui natus est (1).
Pulchra es amica mea (4).*
Pulchrae sunt genae tuae (4).*
Quae est ista (4).*
Quam pulchra es et quam decora (4).*
Quam pulchri sunt gressus (1).
Quam pulchri sunt gressus tui (4).*
Quid habes Hester. Vidi te Domine (3).
Quodcumque ligaveris (6).
Rex Melchior (4).
Salve Regina. Eia ergo advocata (4).
Sancte Paule apostole (1).
Sanctificavit Dominus (3).
Senex puerum portabat. Hodie beata virgo Maria (1).
Sic Deus dilexit mundum (4).
Sicut lilium inter spinas (1).
Sicut lilium inter spinas (4).*
Si ignoras te, o pulchra inter mulieres (4).*
Stella quam viderant magi (1).
Surgam et circuibo civitatem (4).*
Surge amica mea, speciosa mea (4).*
Surge Petre (4).

Surge, propera amica mea (4).*
Surge sancte Dei.   Ambula sancte Dei (4).
Suscipe verbum virgo Maria.   Paries quidem filium (1).
Tempus est, ut revertar.   Nisi ego abiero (4).
Tota pulchra es, amica mea (4).*
Tradent enim vos (3).
Trahe me post te (4).*
Tribulationes civitatum.   Peccavimus (4).
Tu es pastor ovium (6).
Unus ex duobus (1).
Venit Michael Archangelus (1).
Veni, veni dilecte mi (4).*
Videns secundus (4).
Vineam meam non custodivi (4).*
Vox dilecti mei (4).*
Vulnerasti cor meum (4).*

MOTETS FOR SIX VOICES

Accepit Jesus calicem (3).
Assumpta est Maria (6).
Beata Barbara.   Gloriosam mortem (2).
Cantabo Domino in vita mea.   Deficiant peccatores (2).
Columna es immobilis (3).
Cum autem esset Stephanus (6).
Cum inducerent puerum Jesum (6).
Cum ortus fuerit (3).
Deus qui ecclesiam tuam (3).
Dum complerentur dies pentecostes.   Dum ergo essent in unum discipuli (1).
Eia ergo, advocata nostra (7).
Haec dies, quam fecit Dominus (3).
Hic est beatissimus Evangelista (6).
Hic est discipulus ille (6).
Hierusalem, cito veniet salus tua.   Ego enim sum Dominus (2).
Judica me, Deus, et discerne (3).

O bone Jesu (3).
O Domine Jesu Christe (1).
O magnum mysterium. Quem vidistis pastores (1).
Positis autem genibus (6).
Pulchra es, o Maria virgo (1).
Quae est ista (6).
Responsum accepit Simeon (6).
Rex pacificus (3).
Salve Regina, mater misericordiae (7).
Sancta et immaculata Virginitas. Benedicta tu (2).
Solve jubente Deo. Quodcunque ligaveris (1).
Susanna ab improbis. Postquam autem (3).
Tradent enim vos in conciliis (6).
Tribularer si nescirem. Secundum multitudinem dolorum (2).
Tu es Petrus. Quodcunque ligaveris (2).
Veni Domine et noli tardare. Excita Domine (2).
Vidi turbam magnam. Et omnes angeli stabant (1).
Viri Galilaei quid statis. Ascendit Deus in jubilatione (1).

Motets for Seven Voices

Tu es Petrus (1).
Virgo prudentissima. Maria virgo (1).

Motets for Eight Voices
(See also 'Cantiones sacrae')

Alma Redemptoris Mater (6).
Alma Redemptoris Mater (7).
Apparuit gratia Dei (7).
Ave Maria, gratia plena (6).
Ave mundi spes, Maria (6).
Ave Regina coelorum (3).
Ave Regina coelorum (7).
Beata es, virgo Maria (6).

Caro mea vere est cibus (6).
Confitebor tibi Domine. Notas facite in populis (2).
Congratulamini mihi omnes (7).
Dies sanctificatus illuxit nobis (7).
Disciplinam et sapientiam docuit (6).
Domine in virtute tua. Magna est gloria ejus (2).
Ecce veniet dies illa (7).
Etenim Pascha nostrum (6).
Et increpavit eos dicens (6).
Expurgate vetus fermentum (6).
Fili, non te frangant labores (7).
Fratres, ego enim accepi (6).
Haec dies, quam fecit Dominus (7).
Haec est dies praeclara (7).
Hic est panis (6).
Hodie Christus natus est (3).
Hodie gloriosa semper virgo Maria (6).
Jesus junxit se discipulis (6).
Jubilate Deo (3).
Lauda Sion Salvatorem (3).
Lauda Sion Salvatorem (7).
Laudate Dominum in sanctis (30).
Laudate Dominum omnes gentes (2).
Laudate pueri Dominum. Quis sicut Dominus Deus (2).
Magnus sanctus Paulus (7).
Nunc dimittis servum tuum (7).
O admirabile commercium (7).
O bone Jesu, exaudi me (6).
O Domine Jesu Christe (6).
Omnes gentes plaudite (7).
O pretiosum et admirandum convivium (7).
O quam suavis est, Domine, spiritus tuus (6).
Pater noster, qui es in coelis (6).
Regina coeli, laetare (6)
Regina mundi, hodie (6).
Salve Regina, mater misericordiae (6).

Sancte Paule Apostole (7).
Spiritus Sanctus replevit (6).
Stabat Mater dolorosa (6).
Sub tuum praesidium (6).
Surge illuminare Hierusalem (3). *Et ambulabant gentes in lumine* (6).
Surrexit pastor bonus (6).
Tria sunt munera pretiosa (7).
Veni Sancte Spiritus (3).
Veni Sancte Spiritus (7).
Victimae Paschali laudes (7).
Videntes stellam Magi (7).
Vos amici mei estis (30).

MOTETS FOR TWELVE VOICES

Ecce nunc benedicite Dominum (7).
Laudate Dominum in tympanis (7).
Laudate nomen ejus (26).
Nunc dimittis servum tuum (7).
O quam bonus et suavis (26).
Stabat Mater dolorosa (7) (?)[1].

HYMNS FOR FOUR VOICES
(All in Volume 8)

Ad coenam Agni providi.
Ad preces nostras.
A solis ortu cardine.
Aurea luce.
Ave maris stella.
Christe qui lux es.
Christe Redemptor omnium (2 settings)
Conditor alme siderum.

Decus morum dux.
Deus tuorum militum (2 settings)
Doctor egregie.
En gratulemur hodie.
Exultet coelum laudibus.
Hostis Herodes impie.
Hujus obtentu.
Hymnus canoris.
Iste confessor.

---

[1] This is attributed by several writers to F. Anerio.

Jesu corona virginum (2 settings).
Jesu nostra redemptio.
Lauda mater ecclesiae.
Laudibus summis.
Lucis Creator optime.
Magne pater Augustine.
Mensis Augusti.
Nunc jurat celsi.
O lux beata Trinitas.
Pange lingua gloriosi.
Petrus beatus.
Prima lux surgens.

Proles de coelo prodiit.
Quicumque Christum quaeritis.
Quodcumque vinclis.
Rex gloriose martyrum.
Salvete flores martyrum.
Sanctorum meritis.
Tibi Christe, splendor patris.
Tristes erant apostoli.
Urbs beata Jerusalem.
Ut queant laxis.
Veni Creator Spiritus.
Vexilla Regis prodeunt (2 settings).

OFFERTORIES FOR FIVE VOICES
(All in Volume 9)

Ad te, Domine, levavi.
Afferentur regi virgines.
Angelus Domini descendit.
Anima nostra sicut.
Ascendit Deus in jubilatione.
Assumpta est Maria.
Ave Maria, gratia plena.
Benedicam Dominum.
Benedicite gentes.
Benedictus Domine.
Benedictus sit Deus.
Benedixisti Domine.
Bonum est confiteri.
Confessio et pulchritudo.
Confirma hoc Deus.
Confitebor tibi Domine.
Confitebuntur coeli.
Constitues eos principes.
De profundis.

Deus conversus.
Deus enim firmavit.
Deus meus ad te.
Dextera domini fecit.
Diffusa est gratia.
Domine convertere.
Domine Deus, in simplicitate.
Domine in auxilium.
Elegerunt apostoli.
Exaltabo te Domine.
Expectans expectavi.
Illumina oculos meos.
Immittet angelus.
Improperium expectavit.
In omnem terram exivit.
In te speravi.
Inveni David.
Jubilate Deo omnis.
Jubilate Deo universa.

Justitiae Domine rectae (2 settings).
Justorum animae.
Justus ut palma (2 settings).
Laetamini in Domino.
Lauda anima mea.
Laudate Dominum quia.
Meditabor in mandatis.
Mihi autem nimis.
Oravi ad Dominum.
Perfice gressus meos.
Populum humilem.
Posuisti Domine.
Precatus est Moyses.
Recordare mei.

Reges Tharsis et insulae.
Sacerdotes Domini.
Sanctificavit Moyses.
Scapulis suis.
Si ambulavero.
Sicut in holocaustis.
Sperent in te omnes.
Stetit angelus.
Super flumina Babylonis.
Terra tremuit.
Tu es Petrus.
Tui sunt coeli.
Veritas mea.
Vir erat in terra.

LAMENTATIONS FOR FOUR VOICES
(*All in Volume 25*)

Incipit lamentatio Jeremiae Prophetae.   Aleph.   Quomodo sedet.
Vau.   Et egressus est a filia Sion.
Jod.   Manum suam misit hostis.
De lamentatione Jeremiae Prophetae.   Heth.   Cogitavit.
Lamed.   Matribus suis dixerunt.
Aleph.   Ego vir.
De lamentatione Jeremiae Prophetae.   Heth.   Misericordiae Domini.
Aleph.   Quomodo obscuratum est aurum.
Incipit oratio Jeremiae Prophetae.

(There are three other settings: (1) for 4, 5, 6 and 8 voices; (2) for 3, 4, 5 and 6 voices; (3) for 4, 5 and 6 voices.)

LITANIES
(*All in Volume 26*)

Litaniae de B. Virgine Maria inest Ave Maria.   3 and 4 voices.
Litaniae de B. Virg. Maria.   5 voices.

Litaniae de B. Virg. Maria. 6 voices.
Litaniae de B. Virg. Maria. 8 voices (2 settings).
Litaniae deiparae Virginis inest Ave Maria. 4 voices.
Litaniae Domini. 8 voices (3 settings).
Litaniae Sacrosanctae Eucharistiae. 8 voices (2 settings).

PSALMS FOR TWELVE VOICES
(All in Volume 26)

Ad te levavi oculos meos (Ps. 122).
Beati omnes, qui timent Dominum (Ps. 127).
Domine, quis habitabit (Ps. 14).
Jubilate Deo omnis terra (Ps. 99).

ANTIPHON

Salve Regina. 4, 8 and 12 voices.

MAGNIFICATS
(All in Volume 27)

5 Magnificats on the 1st tone.
4 Magnificats on the 2nd tone.
4 Magnificats on the 3rd tone.
5 Magnificats on the 4th tone.
5 Magnificats on the 5th tone.
4 Magnificats on the 6th tone.
4 Magnificats on the 7th tone.
4 Magnificats on the 8th tone.

CANTIONES SACRAE
(All in Volume 30)

Benedictus Dominus Deus. 4 voices.
Illumina oculos (doubtful). 3 voices.
In Domino laetabitur (doubtful). 4 voices.

Laudate Dominum in sanctis.   8 voices.
Miserere mei, Deus.   4 voices.
O quam suavis est.   4 voices.
Vos amici mei estis.   8 voices.

SPIRITUAL MADRIGALS FOR FIVE VOICES
(All in Volume 29)

Al fin, madre di Dio.
Amor, senza il tuo dono.
Anzi, se foco e ferro.
Cedro gentil.
Città di Dio.
Dammi, scala del ciel.
Dammi, vermiglia rosa.
Dunque divin Spiracolo.
E con i raggi tuoi.
E dal letto.
Ed arda ornor.
Eletta Mirra.
E quella certa speme.
E questo spirto.
E, se fur gia.
E, se il pensier.
E, se mai voci.
E, se nel foco.
E tua mercè.
E tu, anima mia.
E tu Signor.
Fa, che con l' acque tue.
Figlio immortal.
Giammai non resti.
Ma so ben, Signor.
Non basta ch' una volta.
Novella Aurora.
O cibo di dolcezza.

O Jesu dolce.
O manna saporito.
O refrigerio acceso.
Orto che sei si chiuso.
Orto sol, che.
O solo incoronato.
Paraclito amoroso.
Per questo, Signor mio.
Quanto più t' offend' io.
Regina delle vergini.
Santo Altare.
Se amarissimo fiele.
Signor, dammi scienza.
S' io non ti conoscessi.
Specchio che fosti.
Spirito santo, Amore.
Tu di fortezza torre.
Tu sei soave fiume.
Vello di Gedeon.
Vergine bella.
Vergine chiara.
Vergine pura.
Vergine, quante lagrime.
Vergine saggia.
Vergine santa.
Vergine sola al mondo.
Vergine, tale è terra.
Vincitrice de l' empia idra.

SPIRITUAL MADRIGAL FOR FOUR VOICES

Jesu, flos matris (30).

SPIRITUAL MADRIGALS FOR THREE VOICES

Jesu, Rex admirabilis (30).   *Jesu, sommo conforto* [1]
Tua Jesu dilectio (30).   *Rex virtutem* [1]

SECULAR MADRIGALS
(All in Volume 28; see also 'Cantiones profanae')

Ahi che quest' occhi.	*Donna, vostra mercede.*
Alla riva del Tebro.	*Ecc' oscurati.*
Amor, ben puoi.	*Ecc' ove giunse.*
Amor, che meco.	*Eran le vostre lagrime.*
Amor, Fortuna.	*Febbre, ond' or.*
Amor, quando fioria.	*Fu l' ardor grave.*
Ardo lungi.	*Già fu chi m' ebbe cara.*
Beltà, se com'.	*Gioia m'abond'.*
Che debbo far.	*Gitene liete rime.*
Che non fia.	*Godete dunque.*
Chiara, sì ch'aro.	*Il dolce sonno.*
Chi dunque fia.	*Il tempo vola.*
Chi estinguera.	*Io dovea ben.*
Com' in più negre.	*Io felice sarei.*
Così la fama.	*Io sento qui d' intorno.*
Così le chiome.	*Io son ferito.*
Da così dotta man sei.	*I vaghi fiori.*
Deh! fuss' or.	*Ivi vedrai.*
Deh or foss' io.	*La cruda mia.*
Dido chi giace.	*La ver l' aurora.*
Dolor non fu.	*Le selv' avea.*
Donna bell' e gentil.	*Lontan dalla mia diva.*
Donna gentil.	*Mai fù più cruda.*

---

[1] Not included in the B. & H. edition.

Ma voi, fioriti.
Mentre a le dolci.
Mentre ch' al mar.
Mirate altrove.
Morì quasi il mio core.
Nè spero.
Nessun visse giammai.
Non son le vostre mani.
O bella Ninfa.
O che splendor.
Ogni beltà.
Ogni loco.
Oh! felici ore.
O me felice.
Onde seguendo.
Ovver de' sensi.
Partomi donna.
Perchè s' annida.
Per mostrar gioia.
Pero contento.
Placide l' acque.
Poscia che.
Pose un gran foco.
Prima vedransi.
Prima vedrassi.

Privo di fede.
Quai rime.
Quando dal terzo cielo.
Quando se loro.
Queste saranno.
Questo doglioso.
Rara beltà.
Rime, dai sospir.
Saggio e santo pastor.
Se ben non veggon.
Se di pianti.
Se fra quest' erb'.
Se lamentar.
Se 'l pensier.
Se non fusse il pensier.
Si è debile il filo.
S' i' 'l dissi mai.
Soave fia il morir.
Struggomi.
S' un sguardo.
Vaghi pensier.
Vedrassi prima.
Veramente in amore.
Vestiva i colli.

CANTIONES PROFANAE
(All in Volume 30)

Amor, se pur sei dio.   3 voices.
Anima, dove sei.   5 voices.
Chiare, fresche, e dolci acque.   4 voices.
Con dolce, altiero ed amoroso cenno.   4 voices.
Da fuoco così bel.   4 voices.
Donna, presso al cui viso.   5 voices.
Dunque perfido amante.   5 voices.

Il caro è morto. 5 voices.
Non fu già suon di trombe. 5 voices.
Quand', ecco, donna. 5 voices.
Se dai soavi accenti. 4 voices.
Voi mi poneste in fuoco. 4 voices.

There are, in addition, 14 works from the archives of the Julian Chapel (Vol. 30); 21 from the archives of the Pontifical Chapel (Vol. 31); 17 from the Vatican Library, including the *XI Esercizi sopra la scala* (Vol. 31); 18 from the archives of St John Lateran (Vol. 31); 2 from the archives of Santa Maria Maggiore (Vol. 32); 12 from the library of the Roman College (Vol. 32); and 52, including the debatable *ricercari* for organ or other instruments, from various collections and libraries (Vols. 30 and 32). Many of these works, however, are doubtful or spurious.

APPENDIX C

Anerio, Felice (c. 1560–1614), chorister in the Papal Choir as a boy, afterwards *maestro di cappella* at the English College in Rome, which he left for the service of Cardinal Aldobrandini. Appointed composer to the Papal Chapel on the death of Palestrina in 1594.

Anerio, Giovanni Francesco (c. 1567–c. 1620), brother of the preceding, in the service of Sigismund III of Poland about 1609, then *maestro di cappella* at the cathedral of Verona and, about 1613, appointed musical instructor at the Seminario Romano and *maestro* of the church of the Madonna de' Monti in Rome.

Animuccia, Giovanni (c. 1500–71), composer born in Florence, studied under Goudimel (q.v.) in Rome and was *maestro di cappella* at the Vatican from 1555 until his death.

Arcadelt, Jacob (c. 1514–c. 1575), Flemish composer who became a singer at the court of the Medici in Florence before 1539, in which year he became singing master to the boys at St Peter's in Rome, entering the college of papal singers the following year.

Asola, Giovanni Matteo (died 1609), composer born at Verona, *maestro di cappella* successively at Treviso and Vicenza.

Barri (or *Barré*), *Léonard,* French composer born at Limoges, pupil of Willaert and singer in the Papal Choir 1537–52. Attended the Council of Trent in 1545 to give advice on church music.

Boccapaduli, Antonio, Italian priest-musician, director of the Papal Choir about 1580.

De la Rue, Pierre (died 1518), French composer, pupil of Okeghem (q.v.), successively in the service of the court of Burgundy, of Charles V and of Margaret of Austria during her governorship of the Netherlands.

Des Prés, Josquin (c. 1445–1521), Flemish composer, pupil of Okeghem (q.v.), became a singer in the Papal Choir at Rome in 1486, having spent some time at various Italian courts before. He was later in the service of the Emperor Maximilian and became provost of the collegiate church at Condé in Hainault, his birth-place, where he died.

East, Thomas (died c. 1608), English publisher who brought out, in London, several works by Byrd and the Elizabethan madrigalists.

Ferrabosco, Alfonso (died 1588), Italian composer settled in England before 1562, father of the greater composer of the same name. Left the service of Queen Elizabeth in 1569 and returned to Italy on leave, which he extended until 1572. In 1578 he left England for good and entered the service of the Duke of Savoy. Died at Turin.

Ferrabosco, Domenico Maria (1513–74), composer born at Bologna, where he was *maestro di cappella* at the cathedral of San Petronio. Appointed to a similar post at the Vatican basilica in 1546 and was a singer in the Papal Chapel from 1550 to 1555. Father of the preceding.

Festa, Costanzo (died 1545), Roman composer, became a member of the Papal Choir in 1517 and later *maestro di cappella* at the Vatican.

Fevin, Robert de, French composer born towards the end of the fifteenth century, became chapel master to the Duke of Savoy early in the sixteenth.

Frescobaldi, Girolamo (1583–1643), organist and composer born at Ferrara, where he studied under the cathedral organist Luzzaschi. He was at Antwerp before 1608, when he was appointed organist at St Peter's in Rome. Left for the service of Ferdinand II, Duke of Tuscany, in 1628, but returned to Rome in 1633.

Galileo, Vincenzo (c. 1533–91), Florentine composer, father of the astronomer, Galileo Galilei, studied music under Zarlino in Venice and became famous as a lutenist. One of the first composers, if not actually the first, to write songs for a single voice. He was also a remarkable theorist and writer on music.

Goudimel, Claude (c. 1505–72), French composer born at Besançon, first appeared as composer in Paris in 1549. About 1557, having become a Huguenot, he went to live at Metz with the Protestant colony there, but about ten years later he left for Besançon, and later for Lyons, where he died in the massacre of the Huguenots.

Le Bel, Firmin, French cleric in the diocese of Noyon, succeeded Mallapert (q.v.) as *maestro di cappella* at Santa Maria Maggiore in 1540 and later occupied a similar post at San Luigi dei Francesi, eventually becoming, in 1561, a singer in the Papal Choir.

Mallapert, Robin, French musician, *magister pueri* at Santa Maria Maggiore for some time before 1539, when he was appointed *maestro di cappella* at San Luigi dei Francesi. Apparently he returned to Santa Maria Maggiore about 1550.

Marenzio, Luca (died 1599), composer born in the neighbourhood of Brescia and Bergamo, of whose career very little is known. He seems to have enjoyed the patronage of several princes and was in the service of the Polish court about a decade before his death. Among his patrons were the Duke of Mantua and Cardinal Cintio Aldobrandini.

Morales, Cristobal (c. 1500–53), Spanish composer born at Seville, where he studied under the cathedral *maestro de capilla,* Fernandez de Castilleja. He was *maestro* at Avila 1526–30 and some time later went to Rome, where he became cantor in the Pontifical Chapel in 1535. In 1545 he was given leave to visit Spain, but did not return, living at Toledo, Malaga and Marchena near Seville.

Okeghem, Jean de (died c. 1495), Flemish composer, was chorister at Antwerp until 1444, in the service of Duke Charles of Bourbon 1446–8 and entered the service of Charles VII of France about 1452. Louis XI appointed him treasurer of the church of Saint-Martin at Tours, where he seems to have died.

Roussel, François (Francesco Rossello), French musician, *magister pueri* at Santa Maria Maggiore in Rome in 1549–50.

Soriano, Francesco (1549–1620), Roman composer, became chorister at St John Lateran in 1564. Studied under various masters, including Palestrina. Was successively *maestro di cappella* at the court of Mantua and various churches in Rome, finally (1603) at St Peter's.

Veccia, Cesare, a pupil of Palestrina, and doubtless a kinsman, since he came from the same town and bore the same family name as Palestrina's mother. He became organist at St Agapit's at Palestrina and died there in 1593.

Yonge, Nicholas (died 1619), singer and musical editor in London, published in 1588 a volume of Italian madrigals with English translations entitled *Musica transalpina*.

Zoilo, Annibale, Roman composer and singer of the middle sixteenth century, *maestro di cappella* at St John Lateran and San Luigi, singer in the Papal Choir 1570 to *c.* 1582.

APPENDIX D

BIBLIOGRAPHY

Baini, G., 'Memorie storico-critiche della vita e dell' opere di Giovanni Pierluigi de Palestrina.' 2 vols. (Rome, 1828.) German translation by Kandler and Kiesewetter. (Leipzig, 1834.)

Brenet, Michel, 'Palestrina.' (Paris, 1906 and 1919.)

Cametti, Alberto, 'Cenni biografici.' (Milan, 1894.)

—— 'Le Case di Giovanni Pierluigi de Palestrina in Roma.' (*Rivista musicale italiana*, 1921.)

—— 'G. P. da Palestrina el il suo commercio di pelliccerie.' (Rome, 1922.)

—— 'Giovanni Pierluigi da Palestrina e le sue alleanze matrimoniali. (*Rivista musicale italiana*, 1923.)

—— 'Palestrina.' (Milan, 1925.)

—— 'Rubino Mallapert, maestro di Giovanni Pierluigi da Palestrina.' (*Rivista musicale italiana*, 1922.)

Casciolini, G., 'La vita e le opere di G. Pierluigi da Palestrina.' (Rome, 1894.)

—— 'Nuove ricerche sul Palestrina.' (Rome, 1923.)

Casimiri, Raffaello, 'Il Codice 59 dell' archivio musicale lateranense, autografo di Giov. Pierluigi da Palestrina. Con appendice di composizioni inedite e dieci tavole fototipiche.' (Rome, 1919.)

—— 'Giovanni Pierluigi da Palestrina: nuovi documenti biografici.' 2 pamphlets. (Rome, 1918 and 1922.)

—— 'Memorie musicali' (*Nota d'archivio*). (Rome, 1924.)

Chrysander, P., 'Das hohe Lied von Palestrina.' (*Allgemeine Zeitung,* Leipzig, 1881.)

Fellerer, K. G., 'Der Palestrinastil.' (Ratisbon, 1929.)

—— 'Palestrina.' (Ratisbon, 1930.)

233

Guzzo, A., 'Il Gregoriano e Palestrina.' (*Rivista musicale italiana,* 1921.)

Haberl, F. X., Prefaces to the various volumes of the complete Breitkopf & Härtel edition. (Leipzig, various dates.)

Jeppesen, Knud, 'The Style of Palestrina and the Dissonance.' Translated from the Danish by Margaret W. Hamerik. (Oxford and London, 1927.)

Pyne, Zoe Kendrick, 'Giovanni Pierluigi da Palestrina: his Life and Times.' (London, 1922.)

Raugel, F., 'Palestrina.' (Paris, 1930.)

Respighi, Ottorino, 'Nuovo studio su Palestrina e l' emendazione del Graduale romano.' (Rome, 1900.)

—— 'Palestrina e l' emendazione del Graduale romano.' (Rome, 1899.)

Schmitz, Eugen, 'Palestrina.' (Leipzig, 1914.)

Wagner, P., 'Das Madrigal und Palestrina.' (*Vierteljahrsschrift für Musikwissenschaft,* 1902.)

—— 'Palestrina als weltlicher Komponist.' (Strasbourg, 1890.)

Weinmann, Karl, 'Das Konzil von Trient und die Kirchenmusik. Eine historisch-kritische Untersuchung.' (Leipzig, 1919.)

—— 'Palestrinas Geburtsjahr. Eine historisch-kritische Untersuchung.' (Ratisbon and Rome, 1915.)

INDEX

INDEX

237

Index